Soar with Confidence

An Executive Coach Reveals Secrets, Lies and Countermeasures —
So You Excel Like Top CEOs and Leaders

Pitch ▪ Lead ▪ Succeed

from PitchPowerFest.com

Tom Marcoux
Executive Coach – Pitch Coach
Spoken Word Strategist
Speaker-Author of 41 books
CEO

A QuickBreakthrough Publishing Edition

Copyright © 2016 Tom Marcoux Media, LLC
ISBN: 0997809841
ISBN-13: 9780997809848

QuickBreakthrough Publishing is an imprint of Tom Marcoux Media, LLC. More copies are available from the publisher, Tom Marcoux Media, LLC. Please write TomSuperCoach@gmail.com

or visit www.TomSuperCoach.com

or Tom's blogs: PitchPowerFest.com   InstaMaxPro.com

This book was developed and written with care. Names and details were modified to respect privacy.

Disclaimer: The author and publisher acknowledge that each person's situation is unique, and that readers have full responsibility to seek consultations with health, financial, spiritual and legal professionals. The author and publisher make no representations or warranties of any kind, and the author and publisher shall not be liable for any special, consequential or exemplary damages resulting, in whole or in part, from the reader's use of, or reliance upon, this material.:

Other Books by Tom Marcoux:

- Year of Awesome!
- What the Rich Don't Say about Getting Rich
- Shine! Don't Let Toxic People Extinguish Your Dreams
- Soar! Nothing Can Stop You This Year
- Time Management Secrets the Rich Won't Tell You
- Connect: High Trust Communication for Your Success
- Emotion-Motion Life Hacks ... for More Success and Happiness
- Relax Your Way Networking
- Darkest Secrets of Persuasion and Seduction Masters
- Darkest Secrets of Negotiation Masters
- Darkest Secrets of Making a Pitch to the Film / TV Industry

Praise for *Soar with Confidence* and Tom Marcoux
• "Executive Coach Tom Marcoux has guided me to my best work over the years. Get his book, *Soar with Confidence,* that reveals his best insights and methods to raise your game." – Dr. JoAnn Dahlkoetter, author of *Your Performing Edge* and coach to CEOs and Olympic Gold Medalists
• "In his work, Tom Marcoux shows you how to be a better communicator, to get people to actually listen to you and believe you, and then act on what you say." – Danek S. Kaus, co-author, *Power Persuasion*

Praise for Tom Marcoux's Other Work:
• "Concerned about networking situations? Get *Relax Your Way Networking.* Success is built on high trust relationships. Master Coach Tom Marcoux reveals secrets to increase your influence."
– Greg S. Reid, Author, *Think and Grow Rich Series*
• "In Tom Marcoux's *Now You See Me*, the powerful and easy-to-use ideas can make a big difference in your business and your personal relationships." – Allen Klein, author of *You Can't Ruin My Day*
• "In *Darkest Secrets of Persuasion and Seduction Masters: How to Protect Yourself and Turn the Power to Good*, learn useful countermeasures to protect you from being darkly manipulated."
– David Barron, co-author, *Power Persuasion*
• "In *Connect*, Tom's advice on how to remain true to yourself and establish authentic rapport with clients is both insightful and reality based. He [shows how] to establish oneself as a credible expert."
- Arthur P. Ciaramicoli, Ed.D., Ph.D., author *The Curse of the Capable*
• "In *Reduce Clutter, Enlarge Your Life*, Marcoux will help you get rid of the physical and mental clutter occupying precious space in your life. You'll reclaim wasted energy, lower your stress, and find time for new opportunities." – Laura Stack, author of *Execution IS the Strategy*
Visit Tom's blogs: PitchPowerFest.com   TomSuperCoach.com

Tom Marcoux

CONTENTS*

* These are highlights. Much more is in this book!

DEDICATION AND ACKNOWLEDGEMENTS

This book is dedicated to the terrific book and film consultant, and author Johanna E. Mac Leod. It is also dedicated to the other team members. Thanks to Barry Adamson II (MyWordsforSale.com) for editing some sections. Thanks to Johanna E. Mac Leod for rendering this book's cover.

Thanks to my father, Al Marcoux, for his concern and efforts for me. Thanks to my mother, Sumiyo Marcoux, a kind, generous soul. Thank you to Higher Power. Thanks to our readers, audiences, clients, my graduate/college students and my team members of Tom Marcoux Media, LLC – and PitchPowerFest.com. The best to you.

Soar with Confidence

You need answers.

How do you get there?

Awareness of lies, countermeasures and secrets.

To play at the top of your game and rise to the top of your industry you need three things: the right questions, the right answers and to shift your perception at will.

This book is designed to help you do that—concisely. No filler.

As an Executive Coach, I'm sometimes called a "thinking partner." In addition to serving as a CEO, leading team members in three countries, *I help my clients cut through and get to the heart of the matter.*

Gerard, a client, asked me, "Why did you write 41 books?"

"It's like I'm a surgeon, and I *made* my scalpel," I replied. "Writing those books was part of refining my own thinking. My clients expect *brief*, insightful coaching. I know when to ask the right question to shake things up and when to listen—and when to say, 'Did you hear what you just said? Use that detail.'"

Ask yourself this question: "What three things do I need to improve in my business?"

This book focuses on *Getting You the Advantages* to take your business to a higher level.

You need to operate on a higher level.

The material is divided into

- Leadership Advantages
- Pitch Advantages*
- Success Advantages

* The sections on "Pitch" are about communicating well to board members, investors, team members and even the media.

To *Soar with Confidence,* to feel real confidence, you learn and use principles for **top level communication** to board members, team members and the media. Every chapter of this book gets straight to the point with **principles, countermeasures and secret methods** that *give you the advantage* in various situations. You experience improved confidence as you empower yourself **to adapt well.**

Let's move forward.

Pitch Advantage

Countermeasure #1: Practice Recovery Methods

Lie: Confidence is a magic pill that eliminates all nervousness.

Countermeasure: Practice Recovery Methods

Secret: "That's been one of my mantras—focus and simplicity. Simple can be harder than complex; you have to work hard to get your thinking clean to make it simple." – Steve Jobs

What is simple and useful? Be genuine.

Some people actually have a fear that if they're genuine then listeners will be able to see their flaws and vulnerabilities.

Instead of carrying some form of fear and dread about that, it's helpful to prepare for potential mistakes. So for years, I have trained clients and graduate students in **Recovery Methods. I teach what to do if one's mind goes blank during a pitch or other form of presentation.**

You can quiet a lot of fearful feelings when you KNOW that you're ready to handle a mistake during a speech.

You'll feel more confident!

I addressed much of this in a blog article (from PitchPowerFest.com):

Give Your Best Speech or Pitch— Do Better than Rehearse!

"It's the most important speech of my life so far," my client Theresa said. "I know I've got to rehearse," she continued.

"You need more than simple rehearsal. You need what I call *Double Power*," I replied.

Double Power so You Shine as You Speak:
- Rehearse Recovery Methods
- Rehearse with a skilled Coach

1. Rehearse Recovery Methods

In some of my current writing, I use the structure of "Lie, Countermeasure, Secret" to briefly get across vital information.

For example:

Lie: Just rehearsing the lines of a speech over and over will give you confidence.

Countermeasure: Rehearse Recovery Methods

Secret: Your nervousness quiets down and your confidence goes up when you're certain that you're ready to adapt to mistakes and problems during a speech.

What's the big fear that a speaker has? Having one's mind go blank!

Here are Three Recovery Methods:

- **Practice Phrases to Buy You Time**

For example, at IBM while I was giving a speech, I said, "I'll need to pause for a moment. My brain needs more RAM." The tech people in the audience really enjoyed laughing at that comment.

- **Say, "At this moment, I want to emphasize—"**

If you lose your place, you can go back to the topic of your speech, and say, "At this moment, I want to emphasize—" This phrase works in two ways: 1) If you're repeating yourself, this is no problem and 2) If you're saying a detail for the first time, the phrase also works.

- **Take a drink of water**

Taking a drink of water is a classic way to give yourself some time to organize your thoughts.

2. Rehearse with a skilled Coach

A skilled Coach will hear what is authentic in you and point it out. My training as a professional speaker (over 15 years, a professional member of the National Speakers Association) and as a trained actor/feature film director/screenwriter, makes me alert to when a speaker is "in the zone." That's when you shine at your best.

Here's the secret about rehearsing with a skilled Pitch/Speech Coach:

The Coach hears your best phrases and points them out to you. Then your speech is tailored to your uniqueness and authenticity. You then have an edge in giving the pitch or speech.

Let's Go further in our conversation about confidence:

I first shared this material (on the W.A.K.E. Process) in my book *The Power of Confidence:*

Where does real confidence begin? With energy.

The source of real energy is your True Self and I'll describe that below. I've trained clients and workshop attendees in the W.A.K.E. Process. (The idea is wake up to the essence of *real confidence.*)

W – want it from your True Self

A - adapt

K – keep learning

E – encourage help

1. Want it from your True Self

What is your True Self? It's the part of you that is

naturally courageous. It's the part of you that longs to grow and focuses on expansion. That's the source of real energy. You want something deep in your heart, and you'll do what's necessary to grow as a person to make things happen.

"It's no use saying, 'We are doing our best.' You have got to succeed in doing what is necessary." – Winston Churchill

What is necessary? Preparation, getting coaching and putting effort into your rehearsals. One of my favorite phrases is: *Courage is easier when you're prepared.*

The energy of your True Self is your source for doing the necessary preparation and rehearsal!

Additionally, Your True Self is connected to your intuition.

Here are the differences between the Voice of Intuition and the Voice of Fear:

Voice of Intuition: Expand, experiment, take an appropriate risk.

Voice of Fear: Contract, hide, take no risks.

To live the life of a confident person, it's necessary for us to connect with our True Self.

"Confidence…requires hard work, substantial risk, determined persistence, and sometimes bitter failure. Building it demands regular exposure to all of these things."
– Katty Kay and Claire Shipman

What empowers you to endure risk and sometimes bitter failure? *Wanting something from your True Self!*

2. Adapt

In my book *Shine! Don't Let Toxic People Extinguish Your Dreams*, I wrote that you "need to prove it to yourself."

The truth is: Setting a small task and accomplishing it truly empowers your confidence on the subconscious mind level.

That's the essence and **value of adapting.** When you adapt on a small level, you prove to yourself you're effective at adapting. You can handle situations that are new and even tough to endure.

Confidence is not comfort.

So where could you take comfort? You can feel stronger when you prove it to yourself that you can adapt.

Focus on learning more and adapting more—and you've started to develop real confidence in yourself.

I always remember this particular definition of self-esteem:

"Self-esteem is the disposition to experience oneself as being competent to cope with the basic challenges of life and of being worthy of happiness. It is confidence in the efficacy of our mind, in our ability to think. By extension, it is confidence in our ability to learn, make appropriate choices and decisions, and respond effectively to change. It is also the experience that success, achievement, fulfillment—happiness—are right and natural for us. The survival-value of such confidence is obvious; so is the danger when it is missing. – Nathaniel Branden

The way you develop real confidence (and self-esteem) is to learn and literally practice adapting to situations in life.

3. Keep learning

"My biggest motivation? Just to keep challenging myself. I see life almost like one long University education that I never had—every day I'm learning something new." – Richard Branson

When you learn, you win even if you do not get the outcome you preferred.

For example, many of us must persuade others in order to

conduct our business. One of my favorite methods comes from top author/consultant/speaker Alan Weiss. If someone declines to hire him, he asks this question: **"Would you take a minute to educate me about what I could have done better to win your business?"**

I've coached a number of clients and audiences with my phrase: "When you're listening, you're winning."

This is an essential part of real confidence: You know that you learn from each endeavor so you're literally getting better every day!

So the truth is: *You're confident that you'll learn from each situation.*

4. Encourage help

"Nothing is impossible for the [person] who doesn't have to do it himself." – A. H. Weiler

When you get coaching you do not have to do something by yourself. You're learning, and you have someone watching your back.

I have my own coach and a number of mentors. Furthermore, I study every day. I read 74 books a year. How? When I trained MBA students two times at Stanford University, the team leader asked, "Tom, do you want to take a speed reading course here?" I jumped at the chance. I walked in reading at 400 words a minute, and the class raised my reading speed to 520 words a minute. (At the time, reading at 600 words a minute did *not* work for me!)

I share the above example to clearly make this point: **Get help! Get coaching. Study and benefit from the wisdom of other people.**

My sweetheart has dyslexia. So she's *listened* to a number of audiobooks. You can turn your car into a "rolling university."

"The man who doesn't read good books has no advantage over the man who can't read them." – Mark Twain

Encourage people to help you. How? First, be kind and friendly. Listen well, and demonstrate that you HAVE been listening. You can say something: "I'm listening carefully to you. It sounds like ____ is most important to you."

Second, keep people posted about how you are doing something good with the guidance that they gave you. When a team member Daniel guided me to improve a project, I *made sure to express appreciation.* I also told other people how Daniel's guidance proved so valuable. This practice encourages my colleagues and team members to offer me appropriate guidance.

In a way, you're giving the person a great reputation (or personal brand) of being a wise person.

So in summary: Confidence is NOT comfort. And the real experience of confidence arises from our life experience, learning and improving through rehearsal.

Remember the W.A.K.E. Process:

W- want it from Your True Self

A – adapt

K – keep learning

E – encourage help

Principle: You develop real confidence when you're prepared to adapt to making a mistake (in a speech for example).

Countermeasure: Rehearse your Recovery Methods.

Power Question: If you're going to give a speech, have you rehearsed Recovery Methods in addition to the text of the speech?

Special Note: The previous section began with material related to pitching and giving a great speech. From this point forward, I am placing the sections into three parts entitled *Leadership Advantages*, *Pitch Advantages*, and *Success Advantages*.

We'll begin with *Leadership Advantages*.

Book 1:
Leadership Advantages

Leadership Advantage #1

The Effective Leader "Protects the Talent" and Guards Momentum

When I have directed feature films, I shared *Two Key Principles* with key crew people. These principles can also help you increase your prosperity, enhance your health and boost your happiness.

The principles are:
1) Protect the Talent
2) Guard Momentum

(The effective leader can make better decisions by memorizing useful principles such as the two noted above.)

1. Protect the Talent
On a movie set, the talent are the actors. I have heard

crew members grumble about how actors can rest in their trailer most of the day. The stand-ins are called to take the position of the lead actors as the director of photography has crew members adjust the lights.

Here's the point. The talent/actors need to be well-rested to perform at their best in the crucial moments when the movie camera is capturing the action.

You, in your own life, are the Talent. You need to be well-rested before you arrive at a meeting, give a speech or perform in a job interview. No one can take your place.

Here's the truth: No one cares as much as you do about what happens in your own life. And, no one else can feel **your intuition's call that moves you toward your destiny.**

So you must Protect the Talent: protect your own personal energy.

On the other hand, my father has sent a mudslide of opinions at me my whole life. But he has never jumped into the adventures I have had: directing and acting in feature films, guest-lecturing at Stanford University, lead singing (and song composing) for a band, and more. My father only knew about his career as a letter carrier ("mailman"). His opinions were like mud that could cause me to slip! So I learned to move forward and listen to My Own Heart.

I invite you to Protect the Talent—that is, protect your own heart. Listen to your intuition. How do you know that it's your intuition? Here's the distinction:

Your Intuition calls you: to expand, experiment, try something new, get coaching, take an appropriate risk.

Your Fear calls you: to contract, hide, avoid an appropriate risk.

Protect the Talent. Protect yourself from dis-empowering opinions. By the way, do get some advice—from someone who has accomplished what you want to do!

As an Executive Coach, I have a distinction: I am a CEO

who helps Leaders Maximize their Influence and Impact. I lead teams in the United Kingdom, India and the United States of America. So I'm not talking from theory. I'm talking from my experience in leading teams since I was 9 years old, making my first film. For example, I directed a feature film that went to the Cannes Film market and gained international distribution. I deeply know about leadership.

[You can see my 1.8 min. video about leadership at YouTube. Type "Tom Marcoux Lead So I Follow"]

2. Guard Momentum

I'll say this in few words: Guard Momentum or Miss Out on Much in Life.

I'm sometimes stunned at how friends and family can actually sabotage your momentum. They may be afraid for you, but they do not realize that your pain and effort are worth it to you!

What's going on here? Your friends or family members do not feel your destiny. They are not comforted by your personal vision. Bluntly speaking, they may not be a similar type of person as you. Some people merely seek comfort.

As an Executive Coach and Spoken Word Strategist, I explain to clients: "Confidence is NOT comfort." If you're feeling some nervousness, that's good. Why? Because you care! As a trained actor and director, I know this: If the actor feels no nervousness before performing tonight's play then he or she does NOT care. Hence, a lousy performance.

Nervousness simply means that you care. What you do is take that energy and convert into your "get ready energy." This "get ready energy" empowers you for preparation before an event.

Along this line, Confidence arises from rehearsal. Through rehearsal, you start to feel it "in your bones" that *you know* that you know!

Here's where "Guard Momentum" comes in:
Once you have momentum going, the universe bends in your favor. Things get done more easily! It's true. For example, the name for one of my blogs came together quickly due to momentum. The ideas flowed, and within 8 minutes, I was certain, and I paid for the Domain Name:

YourBodySoulandProsperity.com (with visitors from 88 countries).

Also . . .

Guard Momentum from your own self-sabotaging habits. Some of us start writing well and then say, "Oh, that's going well; I'll get a cup of coffee." No! Keep with it. Stay on a roll.

On a movie set, the director sets the pace. Every time I direct the crew to move the camera, it's called a "set up." That is, you set up the camera on the tripod or crane. To keep up momentum, I'll design my day of filming so we can quickly film different scenes. For example, I filmed in one direction on a street. Then I had the camera face the other direction, and I filmed another scene (for another section of the film). I kept up a fast pace, and we did many set ups per day.

Clint Eastwood, as a director, is known for doing a lot of set ups in a day. Clint is also known for only filming a couple of takes. His actors (both male and female) know to bring their "A-game" to the first take. It may be the only take they get! All of Clint's films come in under schedule and under budget. And the actors are happier. Clint guards momentum.

When you want more success in your life . . .
1) Protect the Talent

Get enough sleep, exercise, nutritious food and appropriate breaks for yourself.

2) Guard Momentum

Protect yourself from your own self-sabotaging behaviors to hesitate or procrastinate; make daily progress; do not let people talk you out of getting things done.

Some time ago, I was writing book after book. I had a couple of friends who tried to talk me out of writing at such a speedy pace. I'd have 3 editors simultaneously working on different sections of a business book I was writing. Here's the point: None of the naysayers had ever written a book. [Remember, I said, "Get advice from someone who has accomplished what you want to do!"]

By the way, the naysayers were often bellyaching about their lives.

I was having fun in writing the books (even with the hard work involved).

So I wrote 41 books. And two of those friends moved themselves out of my life. What a relief!

When you Protect the Talent and Guard Momentum, you have the opportunity to live in a joyful way.

"When you say you fear death, you are really saying that you fear that you have not lived your true life." – Dr. David Viscott

"People living deeply have no fear of death." – Anais Nin

Some might think the above statements are extreme.

Still, we can see that living with courage and taking appropriate risks form a joy-filled journey.

How will you make today count?

Lie: Just making sure people do their jobs is enough to keep you strong and productive.

21

Countermeasure: Take action to "Protect the Talent" AND Guard momentum.

Secret: "When you recover or discover something that nourishes your soul and brings joy, care enough about yourself to make room for it in your life." – Jean Shinoda Bolen

Principle: Keep yourself strong (Protect the Talent).

Countermeasure: Take action to "Protect the Talent" AND Guard momentum.

Power Question: Are you protecting yourself? Do you guard your time and personal energy? What can you do to take better care of yourself?

Leadership Advantage #2

You're in the Customer-making Business

"So I want to be a speaker. I guess I just have to meet a lot of people and find places to speak," my client Robert said.

"That's part of it. Still, it actually helps if you shift your thoughts to how you're really an 'infopreneur,'" I replied.

"What's that?"

"You're helping people create positive change. You make that happen in a lot of ways. You give speeches; you coach people one on one. You have books, audio programs and online courses. More important than that. You not just trying to sell a speech. You're really looking to create a repeat customer," I explained.

Lie: You're in the [product] business.
Truth: You're in the customer-making business.
Secret: "Make a customer, not a sale." – Katherine Barchetti

Countermeasures:
1) *Make a way to interact with you a "no barrier situation"*
2) *Have a series of steps*

3) *Look at making a customer-for-life*
4) *Look at helping customers so it's easy for them to refer you to others*

1. Make a way to interact with you a "no barrier situation"

If you hold a free conference call each month, you're using a "no barrier situation." That is, you have removed cost, travel and inconvenience from the equation.

2. Have a series of steps

How do people first get to know that you bring value? Do they hear you give a free conference call? Or does one read an article on your blog or posted on LinkedIn? Think of what you offer as a series of steps. The first steps are no cost or low cost like a paperback book. Then one can take a workshop—up to having a private one-to-one coaching session. The series of steps relate to access and fee. The more exclusive the connection, the higher the fee.

3. Look at making a customer-for-life

Repeat business is the backbone of a viable business. In the beginning of my book *What the Rich Don't Say About Getting Rich,* I shared the tragic story of how one of my friends died. Up until his last week of life, he was scrambling for new clients. He wrote press releases. Because the news cycle could make his press releases useless if a celebrity couple broke up (for example), he was leaving a wake of dissatisfied clients.

I talked to him about making customers-for-life. As an experienced journalist, he could have developed a side of his business as a media coach. Then he would have had repeat customers.

Tragically, he died before implementing valuable changes.

But this is NOT for you.

Focus on making a spectrum of services so you create customers-for-life.

4. Look at helping customers so it's easy for them to refer you to others

Some businesses actually have a dedicated webpage so that a happy customer can forward the link. The client who refers gets discounts on products, and the new client also gets a reward "as a friend of one of our happy clients."

See if you can set up such an easy referral process for your own business.

Principle: You're in the customer-making business.

Countermeasures:
- Make a way to interact with you a "no barrier situation."
- Have a series of steps
- Look at making a customer-for-life
- Look at helping customers so it's easy for them to refer you to others

Power Question: Every week are you devoting significant efforts and strategy to making customers-for-life?

Leadership Advantage #3

Shift to Calm on Demand

"Why do you trust Stephanie, the vice president at your company?" I asked.

"Because she holds her calm in a crisis situation," Terri said.

Lie: It's okay to lose your cool in front of the team.

Countermeasure: Train your brain to go to a calm state of being.

Secret: "The heart and soul of the company is creativity and innovation." – Bob Iger, CEO of Walt Disney Company

My addition to Bob Iger's idea is the question: "How do you get to the creativity and innovation? **It's when release yourself from distress, and you get to a calm place.**

To illustrate this, I'll share a speech I was recently called to give. Here is the text of my speech **"Calm Brings the Solution":**

"I'm on the set. I'm directing my first feature film. I'm also playing a leading role in the film so I'm really stressed out.

I'm even more stressed out because the 10-year-old girl portraying the daughter of the main character of the film is not here yet!

It's a tiny budget movie so we can't miss a day. I heard once that Woody Allen said, "We're going home. It's raining. We can't film." Well, good for Woody Allen.

My directing this tiny budget movie was *not* the same situation.

Then, I hear the little girl's name. "Kim is here," says a crew member.

A big smile on my face, I turn around and then my face drops. Because Kim has a broken thumb. Apparently over the weekend, she broke her thumb.

There's no broken thumb in the screenplay! What am I going to do? I can't recast this role. We don't have the budget for an extra day. What am I going to do?

And this leads to the benefit of this conversation: How can you instantly go to calm? How can you get to peace?

My main point is: Calm Brings the Solution.

If you can get yourself to calm, you can get yourself to a solution. And I'll tell you how I got to the solution with Kim and her broken thumb in a little bit.

Here's the thing. I did some research on meditation. Meditation is said to help you and to help you feel better.

According to the research I looked at, meditation can actually change your brain so the left portion of your pre-frontal cortex will change. And there will be more activity.

For example, researchers recorded the brain activity of Buddhist monk Matthieu Ricard's brain. The researchers used 256 sensors on his head and a functional MRI scan.

28

Ricard was recorded as the "happiest man in the world."

I could use some of that. Couldn't you? *[Audience laughs.]*

What does it mean to be the happiest person? It means that your left portion of your pre-frontal cortex has the most activity. That's the part of your brain that focuses on the positive.

There is a way to get to happy, to get to calm. There is a way to get to peace, and it's called meditation.

Unfortunately, I've never been able to sit still for this. I'm just not one of those people who likes to just sit there.

Then I found a book titled *Seven Masters, One Path* by John Selby. From this book, I found that you could get yourself into a meditative state really fast if you do one thing. And we're going to practice this method a little later in our conversation.

The process is to focus on one image and to concentrate on one sound—at the same time. The eyes focusing and the ears focusing will take the ruminating thoughts, the worrisome thoughts, out of your current thinking.

According to the research, your brain will step away from the troublesome thoughts because you're focusing with your eyes and ears at the same time.

On learning this, I went "Wow! That might be for me!"

For a number of people meditation can be quite uncomfortable because you're just with your thoughts. Some of these thoughts you do *not* want to sit with.

Instead, the concentrating on one image and one sound makes the worrisome thoughts go away—and we can have some space and peace.

We have been talking about details from my research:

The brain can be changed. The left side of the pre-frontal lobe can be improved.

This is called neuroplasticity. You can actually change

how your brain is structured.

Prior to my research, I heard "meditation 20 minutes in morning and 20 minutes at night." And I said, "Not for me."

There has to be something in the world that can make a difference.

Then, I read about one image and one sound simultaneously, and I started my own research. For the recent 31 days, I have conducted a research project of my own. For 31 days, every morning before I turn on any electronic devices (because when you turn on the devices, you're gone), I sit down and focus on a plastic candle. And I breathe in and then say, "Ahhhhhhhhhhh." I make this sound.

I'm focused with my eyes on the candle and I'm focused with the sound. More than that, *I'm actually doing something.* I finally found a way for me to calm down by actually doing the breathing.

I mentioned that 20 minutes would not work for me. So I take you to another piece of research. A top proponent of meditation, Ram Dass (born Richard Alpert) was asked, "How long do you meditate?"

He said, "Three minutes a day."

Well, I can do that! I've been doing that for 31 days.

It IS better. It does help.

Now, I invite us—for just 5 seconds to pick any object to look at. A pen on the desk. An item.

And for just 5 seconds, everyone make the "Ahhh" sound. Ready? And begin. *[Audience makes the "ahhh" sound in unison.]*

And let's "complete."

So we can do this for 3 minutes. And it doesn't hurt.

Now, I'll bring this all together.

Calm brings the solution.

So what did I do about the little girl and the broken thumb? Because broken thumbs were not in the script.

I told everyone to "Take 10 minutes" which means everyone take a break.

I sat down. I did some thinking. I got calm, and I realized that I could make the screenplay better.

There are two brothers in this screenplay—my first feature film that I directed. The two brothers don't get along. So I had one brother say to the other brother, "Just in case you're interested, your daughter broke her thumb!"

This made the scene even better.

To bring this all together: **The research shows that you can change the actual structure of your brain by doing some form of meditation. You can actually become happier by meditating.**

We can see, if we put on sensors, that the part of your brain that is positive can become more active. We learn that Matthieu Ricard has affected his brain through meditation. His left pre-frontal lobe of his brain is the most active of anyone *ever* measured.

He probably meditates five hours a day. Forget it—that's not me. Maybe not you, either.

But the point is: We *can* mediate for 3 minutes.

Let's all remember that Calm (just like when I became calm and solved the screenplay problem about the broken thumb) ...

Calm Brings the Solution."

Principle: Calm Brings the Solution.

Countermeasure: Use 3 minutes a day to condition your mind to go to a calm state of being.

Power Question: What are you doing to condition yourself to be calm under crisis situations?

Leadership Advantage #4

Discover the Power of "Lead So I Follow, Speak So I Believe"

How often do you hear someone say something positive about a leader or a manager? Not often. Why? We have some subconscious expectations of what good leaders do. I coined this phrase: "Lead So I Follow, Speak So I Believe."

I have led teams since I was nine years old, directing my first film. I've focused on being a good leader for decades. As a CEO, I currently lead teams in the United Kingdom, India and the USA. I've worked with mentors to develop my leadership skills. Further, as an Executive Coach and Spoken Word Strategist, I guide and support leaders to increase their impact and influence.

"Lead So I Follow, Speak So I Believe" is the experience that I want my team members to have. "I" stands for my team member.

Good leadership is NOT about the leader's ego. It's about making it possible to get things done and to have team members be clear about "the mission and the mighty." By this I mean, the leader shows how the team member can excel and "be mighty."

"Speak So I Believe" is about the team member believing that she CAN succeed. It's also about people believing that the project is worthwhile. No one ever got excited by a leader saying, "Come join us. We're doing something mediocre."

"Speak So I Believe" is about the team member believing that "I can trust this leader."

Nurture dialogue

"Whoever does the most talking has the most fun." – Ruth Reed

Good leadership is not focused on "slick talk." Many of us can see through that. It comes from empowering questions.

When you, as the leader, ask empowering questions, then the team member will have the fun of talking. More than that, you as the leader, will learn a lot about what is going on in your team and in the individual team members.

Use "Headlines" and "Taglines" ("Taglines get the dialogue going.")

An effective leader gives the headline like: "I'm now going to talk about three possible solutions to the XY situation."

Then, the leader shows that she or he is open to input by using a tagline like this: "After I discuss the three possible solutions, I'm going to open this up. I want to hear your ideas, thoughts and feelings."

How do you eliminate miscommunication and confusion?

When you express a headline, the listener understands your point up front.

When you use a tagline, the listener feels comfortable and primed to offer useful ideas for the discussion.

Start in a Positive Manner

As the leader, you set the tone. Do not let loudmouth team members start every meeting as a "complaining fest."

Instead, start a meeting with this question: "Who has an appreciation to mention about someone or something that's working?"

Lie: A leader can just wing it when he or she speaks to team members.

Countermeasure: Prepare your comments well. Work with a coach. Put in spaces in your presentation so you can hear input from your team members.

Secret: "Most of the successful people I've known are the ones who do more listening than talking." – Bernard M. Baruch

Power Questions: How can you add "headlines" and "taglines" to your interactions with team members? How will you do more listening?

Tom Marcoux

Leadership Advantage #5

Make Sure Vital People Get What They Need

The first day of directing my first feature film was surely different than how I'd imagined it to be.

I was bursting with energy and enthusiasm. I felt so grateful to be surrounded by people helping me make my movie!

I'd heard that Walt Disney did not really praise people. In Disneyland, just a few days before opening day, he glanced at a tree on Main Street, U.S.A.

"That should be three feet back," Walt said.

The next day he walked past the same tree. It was moved three feet back. He simply nodded.

That was it. No praise. No thank you.

I resolved to be different than that.

And then I learned something important.

It's not about what makes me feel better.

It's about communicating to people *in the way they can take the message in.*

One particular actor did NOT connect with my enthusiasm.

I learned to give him the bare minimum information. Other actors like to talk and talk.

My point is: **Make sure vital people get what *they* need.**

Lie: You can keep everyone happy and liking you.

Countermeasure: Make sure vital people get what they need.

Secret: "You can help a thousand but you can't carry three on your back." – Jim Rohn

I've learned to be truly selective when hiring people. I do NOT want anyone to "get on my back." By this I'm referring to Jim Rohn's "you can't carry three on your back."

There are some talented people who mean well, but they just do not have it together yet.

I look for people who have these four elements of a good personal brand. I use "T.H.O.R." to keep these ideas memorable: trustworthy, helpful, organized and respectful.

Before I hire someone, I gather data points. Then I can assess whether someone really is trustworthy, helpful, organized and respectful.

I like to ask a person's references this question: "Tell me about something that went wrong and how [the job candidate] handled it."

When someone is on my team, I need to be aware of how each person "needs to be directed in a unique way."

From interviews with successful people, I've learned that "respected" is more valuable than "liked."

One time on the set, as the feature film director, I saw that an actress was not performing well. I whispered to her, "I don't believe you. I don't believe that you care about him.

He's supposed to be the love of your life. You're just angry. That's not what we need. It's better that we can *feel* that you're concerned about him. And you're concerned that your relationship is going to end."

She looked back at me like she wanted to cut me to ribbons with her furious stare.

But the next moment, we rolled the film camera and she had tears in her eyes. Wow! A great performance.

Here's my point. She probably still hates my guts. *I did my job.* I got her where she needed to go.

Also, I whispered to her. I did *not* scold her in front of the crew.

Remember, Make sure vital people get what they need.

Principle: Study each individual. Identify what makes an effective message to that person.

Countermeasure: Aim for respect. Make sure vital people get what they need.

Power Questions: Are you doing what inspires the respect of your team? Are you giving people what they need and NOT anything extra? Do you realize that *brief* is often better?

Leadership Advantage #6

Hire Well and Help People Be "Heroes"

Several years ago, I hear an audio program in which Kenneth Blanchard emphasized that managers need to "catch people doing something right."

I've always remembered that guidance.

People need to know what "a good job" looks like. Helping our team members know what the targets are is part of our job as leaders.

Lie: You can lead anyone to do better.

Countermeasure: Hire well and help people be "heroes."

Secret:" [Great Leaders] start by getting the right people on the bus, the wrong people off the bus, and the right people in the right seats. And they stick with that discipline—first the people, then the direction—no matter how dire the circumstances." – Jim Collins

In the film industry, one wants a "hit movie."

In other situations, a friend will ask, "Was your product a

hit?"

We'll use the H.I.T. process:

H – help them be a hero
I – interview
T – target goals and release resources

1. Help them be a hero

Some people are simply NOT a match for your team. Make sure that you do *not* let them "on the bus." That is, be careful with your hiring processes.

Then you will have the right people on the bus.

Next, you want to help your people "be heroes." By this I mean, *Help them make excellent agreements.*

There has been some research and case studies that reveal that team members do better when they have thought through the situation before they agree that they can complete certain work by a particular deadline.

There are times with one of my team members that I say, "I want you to be a hero. Let's double-check. Is finishing the XY project on Wednesday Oct. 2nd at 4:30 pm realistic for you? Didn't you have the 1-2-3 project review this week, too? If you finish your work early, you're a hero. If you're late, you're *not* a hero."

My team member sometimes replies, "Oh. You're right. It would be more realistic if I say Thursday Oct. 3rd at 3 pm."

The idea here is to make excellent agreements.

Some managers have torpedoed their efforts by trying to bully their team members to move faster.

Instead, people have more commitment when they acknowledge that they have made an agreement.

I will often say, "So I have your agreement that the XY project will be done by you at 3 pm on Thursday, Oct. 3rd at

3 pm?"

"Yes. Thanks for walking me through the process, Tom."

2. Interview

We save so much time when we put more time and effort into hiring well. For example, I was interviewing a new contractor. I saw his portfolio and his work was good, just what we needed. I interviewed his three references. Things looked fine.

But something felt off. When he was slow to return a phone call two times, I said, "Something feels off. It doesn't feel like you really want this work." I did *not* hire him. *I'm so glad.* Upon reflection, I felt that he was going to use up my time by being needy and having some "issues."

One of my mentors said, "Hire slowly; fire fast." His point was that we often know on the gut level that someone needs to be let go. Everyone will be better off: you, your team and the person who knows they're not doing well.

When you have hired a good person be sure "they're in the right seat."

We go back to Jim Collins' quote about people in the right seats on the bus.

Throughout the team member's career in your company, keep "interviewing the person." Ask them, "What do you feel are you best skills? You've been here for a time. How do you see that you better help our team achieve our goals?"

Take what you hear into account as you work with this person.

3. Target goals and release resources

The effective leader ties the team member's personal goals with team goals. That is, if you have someone who wants promotion, then say something like: "Doing well with the XY project will put you in a better position for the next promotion."

One the vital tasks of the effective leader is to help the team member be successful by having the resources she needs.

Be sure that you set patterns in which your direct reports can express what resources they need to successfully complete their assignments.

Principle: Hire well and help employees be "heroes."

Countermeasure: Be sure to keep a good flow of communication so you know what your team members need to successfully complete their assignments.

Power Questions: What do your direct reports need to get their work done successfully? Are your team members the right people on the bus? Does each person have the right seat? Is it wise to have important one-to-one meetings this week so you can get the right people in the right positions?

Leadership Advantage #7

Develop Your Quiet Strength

Every moment of every day someone is looking at you and subconsciously assessing: "Can I trust you?"

Lie: Doing things slowly and methodically always creates trust.

Countermeasure: Prepare and get something done quickly to get things going.

Secret: "Nothing changes until people decide to do the things they must, in order to bring about peace." – Shannon L. Alder

You are called to bring about peace in yourself (see the chapter on "Shift to Calm On Demand"). Furthermore, you're called to inspire trust and peace in those people you lead.

In film making, the skillful director gets her first shot of the day done quickly and efficiently. The answer is put people to work immediately. Have a definite plan and get going.

The cast and crew are watching a first-time director closely. They wonder, "Am I in good hands? Does this person know what she's doing?"

For the smart film director, it helps to pick something simple to do for the first shot:

- The first shot is Jane sits down at this table.
- The first shot is Nick picks up this glass of water.

As a CEO, I lead teams in the United Kingdom, India and the USA. For a graphic novel, I avoid picking the most complicated page to do first. I pick something easier. Then the team can see progress happening fast.

This section is titled "Develop Your Quiet Strength." My point is that your strength is about making decisions. Go forward. You can change something later.

As that first shot is filmed, the director may realize: "No. That won't work. But I won't tell the cast. I'll cut it out in the editing room. No matter. We've begun. And the crew sees that I get straight to work."

Discover the Power of "No Hesitation"

If it's time to lead my team in the design of a website, I tell myself "No hesitation." I write up some first ideas and draw sketches quickly on paper. We've begun. We'll certainly change things as we go. Still, I often don't know how a web page or graphic novel page will look like until I take a mechanical pencil in hand and draw.

Start. Remind yourself that you're safe. You can change it as you go.

Principle: Start now. Remember, "No hesitation."

Countermeasure: Get people into action. You build their trust when you appear decisive.

Power Questions: How are you getting people into action? Are you eliminating times when you look indecisive?

Leadership Advantage #8

Make Sure People Know What the Next Step Is

There's a classic story about how a friend of Henry Ford stormed into his office. "Henry, you're my friend. You know I sell insurance. Why did you buy insurance from that other guy?"

"He asked me," Henry Ford said.

This story reminds us that we need to make sure that people know what the next step is!

Lie: People understand you. Everyone is paying attention and can see the next logical step.

Countermeasure: Make sure people know what the next step is.

Secret: "Ultimately, you're not top of mind to anyone but yourself. When properly understood, this is incredibly freeing and valuable. ... After my umpteenth failure, an incredible realization washed over me: No one cared. No one remembered my mistakes. Here and there, people would have faint memories, but they quickly faded. I was free: free to try hard, fail, learn, rinse, and repeat. I could be reincarnated with each new endeavor." – Brent Beshore, founder and CEO of adventur.es (#28 on 2011 Inc. 500)

Break this habit: assuming that people can see the next step clearly. *You* see the next step because you really care and the next step is "top of mind" with you.

Other people are thinking about a lot of OTHER things.

Here's an example: In the film industry, the next logical step after a screenwriter has met with a producer is to say, "Because I saw that you lit up about how Joe bounces back in the third act, I encourage you to read my screenplay."

You come right out and ask for what you want.

Early in my career, *I was surprised how often people just follow along.*

I remember walking into the director's office at a college where I served as an adjunct professor. I said, "Did you know that Yoda [of *STAR WARS*] speaks in Zen Buddhism sayings? I'd like to teach the Comparative Religion class."

That was the start of 14 years of my teaching Comparative Religion both on campus and online. I wrote the college's online course, too.

"People who ask confidently get more than those who are hesitant and uncertain. When you've figured out what you want to ask for, do it with certainty, boldness and confidence. Don't be shy or feel intimidated by the experience. You may face some unexpected criticism, but be prepared for it with confidence." – *Jack Canfield*

Principle: Clearly express what the next step is to your listener. Ask for what you want.

Countermeasure: Rehearse so well and so often that you're asking for what you want comes out smoothly and confidently.

Power Question: Are you rehearsing how you "ask for the order"? That is, do you smoothly express what the next step is for the listener?

Leadership Advantage #9

Don't Get Stuck in Thinking that You've "Figured People Out"

We may think, at times, that we have people figured out. Then somebody surprises us.

For example, early in my career, I had a lawyer oversee the paperwork to protect my interests in a particular deal. I had emphasized that I was paying the lawyer *one fee* for the whole project. He agreed.

Then what happened? Later, this lawyer came back to me and requested more money beyond the agreed fee. I stood my ground, and the lawyer backed down. (I never worked with that guy again!)

Lie: You've figured people out.

Countermeasures:
- Have sources of accurate information.
- Test, test, test products/brands/marketing campaigns
- Realize that you only have a couple of data-points so far.

Secret: *"What we observe is not nature itself, but nature exposed to our method of questioning." – Werner Heisenberg*

Here's a useful question: Can the person interpret this as a situation in which they have to protect themselves?

I've seen my clients face situations in which they face friends or even family members who suddenly act in harsh ways. Why? Apparently, those opponents think that "they're just protecting their own interests."

So let's look at those countermeasures again:

- Have sources of accurate information.
- Test, test, test products/brands/marketing campaigns
- Realize that you only have a couple of data-points so far.

"Everything we hear is an opinion, not a fact. Everything we see is a perspective, not the truth." – Marcus Aurelius

This quote from Marcus Aurelius reminds us that even when someone purports to give us accurate information, such information can be tinted by that person's own frame of reference.

Whenever possible, seek to have multiple sources of information.

"Truth is stranger than fiction, but it is because Fiction is obliged to stick to possibilities; Truth isn't." – Mark Twain

Principle: Let go of any possible arrogance that you've figured people out.

Countermeasure: Have multiple sources of accurate information. Be sure to access multiple perspectives of a number of people.

Power Question: Who can give you their truthful perspective on what you're working on?

Leadership Advantage #10

Make Victory Blossom from Ashes of Disappointment

What caused the feature film *Ghostbusters* (2016) to lose a reported $70 million at the box office?

Was it because the film was not a hand-off from the original actors to a new cast like *Star Trek* (2009) and *Star Wars: The Force Awakens* (2015)?

Ultimately who knows?

At this point, Ivan Reitman (director of the 1984 original *Ghostbusters*) intends to release animated feature films in this franchise. This just may be a good idea!

Steve Jobs said, *"Sometimes when you innovate, you make mistakes. It is best to admit them quickly, and get on with improving your other innovations."*

Lie: If you're smart enough, you'll avoid big mistakes.

Secret: "Make Victory Blossom from Ashes of Disappointment." – Tom Marcoux

Countermeasures:
a) Get into action.
b) Define victory.
c) Make victory simple (too complex and too long will demotivate people).

1. Get into action

Do something positive. Identify some small step you can take. Perhaps, you want to do a Google search. New ideas can inspire you to make a new combination.

One of the values that a consultant can bring to a company is her experience across a number of companies and industries. Something that may be "standard procedure" in another industry may be just the new pattern for your company.

For example, author Dan S. Kennedy created a new twist on standard direct mail marketing. In a speech, he described how he had a restaurant send out a mailing to 1,000 potential customers in the neighborhood. The second mailing of 600 postcards went to those who did NOT respond to the first mailing. The third mailing went to the 159 people who did NOT respond to the second mailing.

A number of people (clients who work with Dan S. Kennedy) have applied the above pattern to their own business in another industry.

2. Define victory

You could define victory as "take a small step forward." You could gather a subset of your team: the "positive people." You might say, "Okay. I know the reception for the XY project is a disappointment. Let's do some brainstorming here. What small steps can we take forward from here?"

Here's another example. If you lost one major account,

you might define the next victory as "make 30 phone calls and secure 5 first-time appointments." Or you could define the next victory as "call 10 existing clients and invite them to give three referrals each."

Truly, victory can be going into action and taking effective steps forward.

3. Make victory simple (too complex and too long will demotivate people)

Above I identified a couple of simple actions. You're already hurting (and your team may be hurting) so it can be helpful to make the next victory a "short hurdle."

If 30 calls are daunting, how about five phone calls for today?

Principle: Make Victory Blossom from Ashes of Disappointment.

Countermeasure: Identify simple actions so that you can have a victory soon!

Power Question: What simple actions can give you a victory soon?

Leadership Advantage #11

Use Leverage with the Questions You Ask

"Which URL works better Instamax.me or Instamax.biz?" I asked a number of insightful people who are part of my inner circle.

The answers split between the two alternatives.

But then a good friend said, "When I get email, I don't trust unusual URLS. I won't click on them. A .com URL seems substantial."

In that moment, I realized that my friend had shown me a failing of my question. I had limited my options in saying .me or .biz.

My friend gave me the *real, important detail* about which URL invites people's trust. (Our solution: InstaMaxPro.com)

When I say, "Use Leverage with the Questions You Ask" I mean get the most value. In fact, leverage is about investing a small effort and getting a big, useful result.

Lie: Questions tend to get neutral responses. Just asking "why?" will not taint the answer you get.

Countermeasure: Prepare questions strategically. Consider

asking "what?" and "how?" questions.

Secret: "People sometimes think that technology automatically gets better every year. But it actually doesn't. It only gets better if smart people work like crazy to make it better." – Elon Musk

What do smart people really need to do? Ask better questions!

For example, I prefer to show two versions of a cover of a book. Then I ask, "Which of these books would you pick up in a book store or on Amazon.com—if you were looking for a book for yourself or a friend?"

Asking this question is part of what I call *Choice Market Testing*.

I follow up with this question: "What about your preference grabs your attention?"

I often prefer to ask "what?" or "how?" instead of "why?" My reasoning is that people often make stuff up when confronted with the "why?" question. They want to sound reasonable. I suggest that, upon hearing "why?" they jump out of their heart and jump into their head and make something up.

The wise choice is often to focus on asking "what about your preference means more to you?" or some similar question.

Principle: Design your questions to get valuable information and simultaneously attempt to avoid skewing the responses that you get.

Countermeasure: Try different questions and observe how effective the questions are working for you.

Power Question: Are you casual about the questions that you ask? Are you asking questions in a way that subconsciously steers what you hear in response? Are you, perhaps, afraid to hear certain answers so you're failing to ask the crucial questions?

Leadership Advantage #12

Help the Team "Ride through The Desert"

"It's not working," my illustrator, Sandy, said.

"True. And that's part of the process. It doesn't work. And we don't feel good. Until after a number of versions, it DOES work. We just hang on through the desert," I assured her.

Lie: There is a way to avoid the desert in which people feel that a project is (temporarily) a disaster.

Countermeasure: Keep measurements of incremental progress.

Secret: "Every single Pixar film, at one time or another, has been the worst movie ever put on film. But we know. We trust our process. We don't get scared and say, 'Oh, no, this film isn't working.'" – John Lasseter

When a project is not working, have measurements that show that incremental progress is going on. For example, my team is working on the design of a submarine for my graphic novel series, *Jack AngelSword*. We can keep count of how many different sketches are drawn. It could rise to 20 sketches by three different artists—60 sketches. Okay. That may be the process.

Assure yourself and your team that the answers are on their way.

I've noticed that the situation often feels a bit hopeless—and then when the design answer arrives, it's easy to say, "Yes! That one is *exactly* what we were looking for!"

Principle: Assure yourself and team members that the process just calls for hanging on through many iterations.

Countermeasure: Keep measurements of incremental progress.

Power Question: What can you measure in terms of activity in a positive direction?

Success Advantage #13

Get Skilled about Fear

"I know that I need to make those calls," my client Sharon said.

"Which ones in particular?" I asked.

"The calls to the local TV station, radio stations, newspapers ..."

"And what's going on for you?"

"I'm ... I'm afraid," she said.

"That's a good place to start," I said.

"How can that be?"

"When you pull the fear out of the darkness, it gets smaller. We can work on this. We can break the steps down. Courage is easier when you're prepared," I assured her.

Lie: You'll rise to a point that fear won't enter your week.

Countermeasure: Learn to quiet down fear. Do not wait for the total absence of fear. Take action in a positive direction.

Secret: "Inaction breeds doubt and fear. Action breeds confidence and courage. If you want to conquer fear, do not sit home and think about it. Go out and get busy." – Dale Carnegie

There is a fiction that many of us hold: Successful people

somehow erase fear from their daily lives.

"I feel fear really strongly. It's quite unpleasant. ... I don't have a fear of failure. I'm not going to fail to do something just because I fear that I wouldn't win ... I think people often are irrational about fears. ... I thought I had an obligation to do everything possible to make Tesla and SpaceX succeed because I think they're important to the future of the world. And I don't want to have to look back on that and say, 'Well, you know, there's one thing I could have done and I didn't do it and maybe if we had done that we would have succeeded.' I didn't want that to be the case." – Elon Musk

Become Skilled in Quieting Down Fear

The solution is to quiet down fear. Do NOT let fear stop your incremental progress.

"Fear is static that prevents me from hearing myself."
– Samuel Butler

We'll use the N.E.W. process:

N – nurture your strength

E – engage your True Self

W – Work through pain

1. Nurture your strength

It's easier to give into fear when we're physically tired or weak. So a prime defense against fear is to systematically strengthen yourself. How are you doing in getting enough sleep, exercise, and appropriate nutrition? Are you taking appropriate breaks so you come back to work strong and refreshed?

You further strengthen yourself through excellent coaching. You learn how to do things in a better way and you have someone watching your performance so that you become more skillful. You can get coaching in many areas:

public speaking, decision-making and more.

Courage is easier when you're prepared. Take action to devote time and effort to prepare well.

2. Engage your True Self

Your True Self is that part of you that is naturally courageous and brilliant. Your True Self is the source of your real energy to make things happen. When you want something from your True Self, you have a big supply of energy and focus.

"Courage is not the absence of fear but rather the judgement that something is more important than fear." – Meg Cabot

3. Work through the pain

Let's face this together: Much of fear is about pain. Sometimes, we think we will not be able to endure the pain of rejection, disappointment or embarrassment.

From interviews with successful people, I've learned that they have faced rejection, disappointment and even embarrassment so many times that it is not such a big deal. That is, successful people know that they can endure and adapt.

How can you endure pain? We go back to the first step "nurture your strength."

In important ways, **you're faced with a choice: the pain of regret or the pain of proper rehearsal.**

I tend to rehearse every day. That's not an exaggeration. I'm preparing for my next speech or I'm working on new material.

On a number of occasions, I have been asked, "Tom, why have you written 41 books?"

"It's like I'm a surgeon and I've *made* my scalpel. The surgeon needs his scalpel to heal the patient. And my executive coaching client needs me to be *brief* and insightful," I have replied.

"In writing those books, I've boiled down my studies into concise sentences. People today need profound ideas spoken in a BRIEF manner."

I continued, "Furthermore, I need to study and refine my thinking so my clients get the benefit of my agile mind. As an executive coach, I provide an informed point of view that the client wants to augment their own view," I concluded.

"[People] are not afraid of things, but of how they view them."
– Epictetus

So how do you view rejection, disappointment or embarrassment? Do they appear to be a disaster that you can't endure?

"There's a four letter word you must use when you get rejected ... next." – Jack Canfield

Jack would know: He and his partner Mark Victor Hansen endured 140 rejections until their book *Chicken Soup for the Soul* found its home with a publisher.

My idea is: *Make Victory Blossom from Ashes of Disappointment.*

When you hold this idea, you're ready for disappointments. You know that you will rise like the phoenix—stronger, wiser and better.

How do you make victory blossom? You gather your team and you gear up for the next assault on the mountain. You have more information now. So your next meeting or sales call or product will be better-planned and improved.

Principle: Quiet down fear. Prepare so you can handle rejection, disappointment or embarrassment and come back stronger than ever.

Countermeasure: Make sure to nurture your strength.

Power Question: How do you strengthen yourself daily?

Leadership Advantage #14

Have a System to Challenge
Your Assumptions

"They're not getting it," Mark thought. In leading his own company, he thought if he would just emphasize the right details and say it again team members would get more done.

I told him, "You may NOT be the best facilitator of the meeting." The point was: I saw people avoid saying something that seemed to contradict Mark's point of view.

This sometimes happens with a so-called strong leader.

However, a more *effective* leader gets access to a spectrum of ideas. Often, tough news is exactly what we need to excel.

Fortunately, Mark was wise enough to try a new approach. Having another person lead meetings helped him get the most from his team. It also encouraged his team members to think out of the box.

Lie: If you just take the time, you can use reason to always make the right decisions.

Countermeasure: Realize you cannot see what you cannot

see. Have a system to challenge your assumptions.

Secret: "It ain't what you don't know that gets you into trouble. It's what you know for sure that just ain't so."
– Mark Twain

"What do you do as an executive coach?" my friend Adam asked.

"I help my client get what she or he wants. Sometimes, that means I have to shake the person up," I replied.

I continued, "I am in the business of *transformation*. I am not in the business of Band-Aids. I tell a CEO that I'm not your employee. Employees and family members have agendas. Family members can hold to ideas of 'don't change. Don't become inconvenient for me.' I'm here to help you get what you want. I'm do not act like a friend afraid to rock a friendship. I help you see what you need to see so you can create what YOU want to create. That is my agenda. That is my goal."

Often strategy and intense realism is called for.

I call myself an OptiRealist. I'm optimistic that we can do something to improve situations, AND I'm realistic that facing hard facts and using strategy are vital.

Here is the realism part. Let's look at these statements:
- I expect people to protect themselves.
- I expect people will often be short-sighted.
- People will do more to avoid pain than to gain pleasure.
- Each person has blindsides.

Do these statements seem cynical? Case histories and research studies demonstrate that the above statements reflect reality.

"We generally change ourselves for one of two reasons: inspiration or desperation." – Jim Rohn

I ask my clients the tough questions including:

- What truth do you need to face?
- Are you numb?
- Are you all in or not?

How do you challenge your assumptions? Have people who can tell you the truth. Ask yourself the tough questions.

- Am I fooling myself?
- Who can give me a different perspective—that can disagree with my first guess?

Be careful to avoid shooting down ideas that disagree with your own too fast. If you chastise and ridicule a team member for an idea, you're teaching that person to never offer an unusual idea again.

Learn to hear the idea and not have a reflexive critical comment.

There are times when I say, "I'll going to ponder that for a while." That's my way of letting an idea sit for a while. The idea may be strange or not usable on first glance. But the idea may bring a springboard to new and better methods.

Principle: You cannot see what you cannot see.

Countermeasure: Have a System to Challenge Your Assumptions.

Power Questions: Who around you can "tell truth to power?" That is ... who will tell you the truth even if it will shake you up?

Tom Marcoux

Leadership Advantage #15

Watch Out! You May Be Rewarding the Wrong Thing

Author Bonnie L. Gallup tells the story of a CEO who would step into the building and walk down the same row of cubicles every day. Soon employees were becoming jealous of the people on the CEO's route toward his office. They thought that the CEO considered these people to be special. For one thing, the CEO said good morning and talked with these people.

This CEO was rewarding some people with his attention and he was depriving other employees at the same time.

This is my inspiration for the idea: "Watch Out! You May Be Rewarding the Wrong Thing."

Lie: As a leader, you can just go about your day in a "normal way."

Countermeasure: Pause. Go over the elements of your routine with someone you trust. Pay attention to who you are rewarding and for what actions.

Secret: "What gets measured, gets done. What gets rewarded, gets repeated." – John Schnatter (founder of Papa John's)

Let's face it. We reward people all the time. With what? With our attention and with our listening to them.

If we fail to listen to team members, we're actually doing something counter to rewarding them. We basically showing how we do *not* care about these people. Bad move!

As a graduate school instructor, teaching an online course, I keep a grid that shows me how many times I have replied to each student in the discussion topics area.

Every comment is being observed by all the students in the class.

If I reply to a few students' comments more than others, the other students can get jealous.

Instead, it's important for me to keep a log of my own behavior.

Now it's your turn. What behavior are you doing and how might it be seen as you rewarding only a subset of your employees/team members?

Principle: People watch the leader's actions and draw conclusions about who he or she is rewarding.

Countermeasure: Pause. Talk over your routine with someone you trust. Identify how you may be seen as rewarding a certain subset of team members.

Power Questions: Who are you rewarding with your time and attention? [For example, some CEOs make the mistake of putting most of their attention on underperformers and simultaneously ignoring the "super-competent" team members. Bad move!] How can you make sure to pay attention to all team members in turn?

Leadership Advantage #16

Take Appropriate Risks;
Have Multiple Criteria

"We failed," my friend Marina said.

"How?" I asked.

"The film didn't make any money."

"Is that all you wanted to accomplish?"

"Well … "

In an extended conversation, Marina identified these criteria for the film project:

- Move the crew's and actors' careers forward
- Make a film that inspires the audience to have courage and make good things happen
- Make money

"Oh. We did get two out of three," Marina said.

"What about the money part?"

"We went with a distributor who cheated us," Marina said. "I'm definitely going to have plans in place to protect us next time."

"Excellent. You're learning."

Lie: Pick only one objective.

Countermeasure: Have multiple criteria for what you can accomplish with a project.

Secret: "Don't wait for someone to give you permission. Just do it yourself. Find people of like mind. Make movies; tell stories. Do short form; do long form. You're developing this mixed bag of skills that gets you ready for when that break does happen."
  – Jon Favreau, film director of the blockbuster, Iron Man

Use these questions to build your plan for identifying appropriate risks:
  - Will I grow?
  - Will I learn?
  - Will I make new alliances?
  - Can I avoid "losing the store"?
  - Can I make money all the while?
  - Does my heartfelt intuition call me to go forth in this direction?

The top successful people I've interviewed demonstrate that they often use intuition. Intuition is like a muscle: If you don't use it, you lose it.

You need to both make space for your intuition, and you need to take action upon your intuition. Intuition is like a friend who says, "You don't listen to me anyway; I'll just shut up."

Instead, honor your intuition.

First, identify which internal voice you're listening to:

Voice of Fear: contract, hide, don't take appropriate risks.

Voice of Intuition: expand, experiment, grow, take appropriate risks

Second, find a way to take some steps forward. Monitor your results. Check in with your intuition again and again along the way.

The thing about intuition is: Intuition gives you Steps 1, 2, 3. You cannot see Steps 18, 19, 20 yet. Still, at Step #3, you can see the next steps of 4, 5, 6. Your perspective has shifted. It's like you've reached the peak of a small mountain, and you can now see other mountain peaks. Intuition will give you the next steps to take.

Keep stepping forward.

Principle: When assessing a risk, identify multiple criteria for good results.

Countermeasure: Prepare that any project may not yield ideal results but still place your company in a better position.

Power Questions: What are seven positive results that can result if you complete a particular project? Do these results mean more than the possible problems or disappointments that may occur?

Leadership Advantage #17

Create an Environment that Works

Sam tripped over a cord and exclaimed, "Damn! George, I asked if we could have the cords bunched up and placed to the side here."

"You're not very agile are you?" George asked.

This started an argument which wasted time.

Lie: It's okay to only focus on sales measures and ignore work environment details.

Countermeasure: Come up with criteria for how people can best interact and foster cooperation and productivity.

Secret: "You can create the environment you work in. Who is in your crew. Who is in your cast. And you can create an environment that is conducive to creativity and quality of life. And if you can stack the deck in that way, you're more likely to enjoy yourself and end up with a product that everyone is proud of."

– Jon Favreau, feature film director of Iron Man *and* The Jungle Book (2016)

Here we'll talk about two elements of the productive work environment.

a) Interactions that bring up the free sharing of ideas
b) Physical set up of the work environment conducive to creativity and productivity.

1. Interactions that bring up the free sharing of ideas

Steven Spielberg said, "A good director knows when to say yes." For decades I've used that as the springboard to my addition: "A good director sets an environment where there is a lot to say yes to."

I make sure that I hear team members out about how we can improve our projects. I also make certain to let team members know when an improvement is implemented based on a team member's idea.

For example, a team member suggested something new for my series of graphic novels titled *Jack AngelSword*. She suggested that an area of the airship have open walls.

I had never thought of that idea before. We implemented it, and now the design is more thoughtful and adds to the interaction of the characters in that part of the airship.

Improvements in design and characters are celebrated in my team.

How about your team? Do people feel free to offer new ideas?

2. Physical set up of the work environment conducive to creativity and productivity.

Steve Jobs had certain criteria for setting up the new building for Pixar employees. The building needed to foster unplanned meetings between team members.

Jobs said, "If a building doesn't encourage that, you lose a lot of innovation and the magic that's sparked by serendipity." He continued, "So we designed the building to make people get out of their offices and mingle in the central atrium with people they might not otherwise see."

John Lasseter (Chief Creative Officer of Pixar) noted, "Steve's theory worked from day one. I kept running into people I hadn't seen for months. I've never seen a building that promoted collaboration and creativity as well as this one."

Principle: Attention to details that make the work environment more creative and collaborative spark true productivity and innovation.

Countermeasure: Talk with key people about your goals for the group's creativity. Identify how the environment helps or hinders such creativity

Power Questions: How is the environment functioning for the people on your team? Do they feel energized to collaborate and increase creativity? Perhaps, consider having a discussion on this topic. See if you can implement even a small change in a positive direction.

Leadership Advantage #18

Take an Effective Approach to Risk-taking

Google+, at the time of this writing, has implemented a new interface. I do NOT like it. I keep pressing "Back to Classic Google+".

Still, this is smart on Google's part. They're offering me something new. They're not forcing me to accept this new interface yet. But what they're doing is trying out something new under real conditions.

This reminds me of another group that slammed a new name and rebranding on its members. There was a huge outcry, and that group's leadership had to backpedal and drop the initiative. (I'm not naming this group because I know a number of members, and they're still bristling over the experience.)

It's true that for every change there will be dissenters.

Still, when something affects a whole group of people, **it often works better to involve people in the process.**

This reminds me of author John C. Maxwell's advice about having "the meeting before the meeting." He advises that one go to the most influential people in the group and meet with them before the crucial general meeting.

Lie: It's okay to stay with what you've always done—or just plow ahead and dump a big change on people without notice.

Countermeasure: Be sure to have a series of "meetings before the meeting" so that you have key influencers' buy in.

Secret: "The meeting before the meeting helps you to receive buy-in. ... If you deliver surprising news to a group of people and the most vocal and most influential react negatively, the entire group is likely to be negative. ... That's why you want to get those vocal and influential people to buy in ahead of time."
– John C. Maxwell

A lot of books extol the virtue of taking risks. Certainly taking appropriate risks is necessary in business.

"Move fast and break things. Unless you are breaking stuff, you are not moving fast enough." – Mark Zuckerberg, founder of Facebook

"The biggest risk is not taking any risk... In a world that's changing really quickly, the only strategy that is guaranteed to fail is not taking risks." – Mark Zuckerberg

Still, I appreciate John C. Maxwell's measured approach of getting buy in from key influencers before a surprising announcement.
Remember to have "the meeting before the meeting."

Principle: People often react negatively to something that takes them by surprise.

Countermeasure: Be sure to have a series of "meetings before the meeting" so that you have key influencers' buy in.

Power Question: Who are the key influencers in the group that you lead? How will you schedule the "meeting before the meeting" with key influencers? How will you rehearse before each crucial meeting? Will you work with a coach?

Tom Marcoux

Book 2:
Pitch Advantages

Pitch Advantage #1

Unleash Your Real Charisma
When You Pitch

It was the third time that Harry had the investors in the room laughing. This pitch was going well.

As I looked around the room, I could see the smiles on the investors faces.

It reminded me of the comment:

"Among those whom I like or admire, I can find no common denominator, but among those whom I love, I can: all of them make me laugh." – W. H. Auden

I'm NOT saying that you must be able to make investors laugh to gain funding. What *does* really help is that you set them at ease.

You can do that by expressing your own form of charisma.

Lie: If you're an introvert or you're not naturally funny, you have no way of expressing charisma.

Countermeasure: Find your own natural form of charisma and play to your own strengths.

Secret: "Being a leader gives you charisma. If you look and study the leaders who have succeeded, that's where charisma comes from, from the leading." – Seth Godin

I first shared my thoughts on **3 Forms of Charisma** in my book *Darkest Secrets of Charisma.*

Here's a brief summary:

Natural Charm Charisma includes things you can naturally do to make people comfortable in your presence. Your goal is to get obstacles out of your way (like nervous hand gestures) and let your natural charm shine through. *The image: Take a cover off a glowing light bulb.*

Warm Trust Charisma includes things you can do so that people feel that you're genuine and trustworthy. It's all about a warm connection. *The image: Your hand extends in friendship.*

Magnetic Charisma (or Force of Nature) is overwhelming attractiveness. *The image: A magnet pulls people in.*

You can improve upon your situation whether you're already comfortable talking to new people or not.

Charisma does NOT mean

— You must be an extrovert.

— You use words perfectly.

— You copy others who possess charisma.

Instead, you learn to *unleash the charisma power that already resides in you*. When you take action to radiate charisma, you'll get a bonus: You'll feel confident.

In other words, *you act your way to feeling empowered*.

Some people hear the word "act" and think of actors and childhood games of pretending. Drop the idea of pretending. I'm talking about taking action that actually changes your brain. There's a scientific name for this: Neuroplasticity.

The Merriam-Webster Dictionary defines this term as follows:

Neuroplasticity: Capacity of neurons and neural networks in the brain to change their connections and behavior in response to new information, sensory stimulation . . . . Neuroplasticity occurs when neurons in the brain sprout and form synapses. As the brain processes sensory information, frequently used synapses are strengthened while unused synapses weaken.

When you take action, you get new sensory information both from outside and inside yourself. And as we see above, you change your brain as new synapses form. You'll use this book to change how you go about your daily life. So, in essence, this is not merely a book that you read; *it is a book that you do*. Specifically, you learn to **control your actions and amp up your charisma**

Helping my clients amplify their natural charisma is a big part of what I do as both Executive Coach and Spoken Word Strategist.

In my role as Pitch Coach, I help the client find the words that naturally come out of his or her mouth that truly support the person's cause.

For more on charisma, see my book *Darkest Secrets of*

Charisma. Here I'll emphasize these examples:

- My client Nancy has *Natural Charm Charisma* of a great listener. So I help her create more dialogue in her pitch.
- My client Adam has *Warm Trust Charisma.* So I advise him to circulate with investors BEFORE he gives a pitch so he has friends in the audience before he formally pitches.
- My client Jerry has *Magnetic Charisma (or Force of Nature).* I advise that he *avoid* creating needless resistance in the room. Where can such resistance arise? His "smoothness" might be interpreted by some viewers as arrogance. It's best that he carefully selects his words so he does **not** overly play up his achievements. He can *sincerely communicate his gratitude* for his opportunities and how he's *dedicated* to making a contribution to people's lives.

Principle: Play to your strengths. Find your natural form of charisma and accentuate that.

Countermeasure: Let go of your preconceptions of what charisma is and consciously get better at expressing your natural form of charisma.

Power Question: What is your "go to" form of charisma? How can you play to your strength? Will you get a coach to amplify your best practices related to expressing your charisma?

Pitch Advantage #2

How You Can Pitch and Connect Quickly with Investors

"No. That's not how it works in the film industry," the guy giving the pitch said.

I saw the face of the potential investor. He was upset that he had been quickly shut down and given a lecture.

This was no way to get a Silicon Valley Tech investor to invest in one's feature film—no matter what one's status in the film industry was.

This occurred at a private meeting in Palo Alto, California. I felt compassion for people failing to deliver pitches that worked. Seeing these mistakes inspired me to write the book *Darkest Secrets of Making a Pitch for Film and Television.*

Lie: If you're the expert, you'll impress people by quickly shutting them down and proving your expertise.

Countermeasure: Show respect and be a guide not someone delivering a stern lecture.

Secret: "The greatest good you can do for another is not just to share your riches but to reveal to him his own."
– Benjamin Disraeli

How do you win someone's trust? You listen to him or her. You show respect of one colleague for another.

Let's return to the situation with the guy delivering a pitch.

The potential investor says something that's incorrect.

The savvy, effective pitch-maker says:

"I hear you, Paul. I see how that pattern can work in many industries. In fact, that's the logical way to go. And, I can add that it can often work when we …"

We see a number strategic details above:

- "I hear you, Paul" makes it personal and that you're being respectful.
- "That's the logical way to go" delivers a compliment and an acknowledgment.
- "And" is helpful because saying "but" makes it sound like the pitch-maker was telling a lie.

How does "but" make something seem like a lie? Here's an example: "You're a good kid, but your room is messy." The message is: "The truth is you cannot be a good kid while you have a messy room."

"And" implies that multiple true things can be going on. You can see it here: "You're a good kid. And, your grandma gets here in one hour. Please straighten up your room. I know how you two like to sit at your table in your room."

Use the Power of "I agree"
When possible and when you can do it sincerely, say, "I agree." I learned this method from clinical hypnotherapist

and author David Barron.

How can saying a sincere "I agree," be helpful? Perhaps, you've noticed that many individuals spend much of their time trying to prove they are "right."

When you say, "I agree," you *reduce tension in a conversation* and the other person can relax because they do *not* have to prove their point.

In summary, create trust with "I hear you," "And" and "I agree."

Principle: Show respect and be a guide not someone delivering a stern lecture.

Countermeasure: Create trust with "I hear you," "And" and "I agree."

Power Question: When are you going to rehearse and incorporate (for your pitch) "I hear you," "And" and "I agree"?

Pitch Advantage #3

Structure Your Pitch Effectively

It was the fourth pitch in a row that our group heard that evening. No! Not again. I watched the faces of the investors. No connection. The fourth person also failed to get funding. All four people made big errors. (This shook me up so much that I ended up writing a book *Darkest Secrets of Making a Pitch for Film and Television*.)

Lie: You just have to make a concise pitch and get the words perfect.

Countermeasure: Prepare more than the text of your pitch. Learn how to make a real connection with investors.

Secret: "Having a conversation with the investors is important. But everybody just wants to talk [pitch]." — Frank Greene, *venture capitalist, Silicon Valley technology pioneer*

P – prepare your Mirror Neurons
I – interview them (if possible)

T – target answers to "Worst Questions"
C – conduct "dialogue"
H – help them say "yes"

1. Prepare your Mirror Neurons

Researchers have noted that when a person observes another person doing an action, the same neurons (brain cells) are stimulated in the observer's brain.

In his book, *Social Intelligence*, Daniel Goleman, wrote: "The human brain harbors multiple mirror neuron systems, not just for mimicking actions but also for reading intentions, for extracting the social implications from what someone does, and for reading emotions."

Goleman continued, "Mirror neurons make emotions contagious. Letting the feelings we witness flow through us, helping us keep in sync and follow what's going on. We feel others in the broadest sense of the word: sensing their sentiments, their movements, their sensations, their emotions as they act inside us."

You can use this connection to your advantage when you pitch. That is, you can make this work for you if you prepare properly and thoroughly.

You prepare your mirror neurons to serve you and your project by:

a) Rehearsing Recovery Methods
b) Preparing and rehearsing for the "Worst Questions"
c) Rehearsing so that you conduct a "dialogue" at crucial moments

These three actions ultimately enhance your confidence. When you're confident, the investors pick that up. They become confident in you.

1. Rehearsing Recovery Methods

In the previous section, we discussed the process of preparing and rehearing your Recovery Methods. Here I say that memorizing your Recovery Methods gives you a higher level of confidence. You *know* you're ready if your mind goes blank!

2. Preparing and rehearsing for the "Worst Questions"

"T" of "P.I.T.C.H." is "target answers to Worst Questions." So I'll save my comments about this for a few paragraphs beyond this point in this book. Here I emphasize: When you're ready with answers to the toughest questions, you're more prepared and confident than a significant number of presenters. You have a competitive edge.

3. Rehearsing so that you conduct a "dialogue" at crucial moments

You conduct a dialogue by asking skillful questions and incorporating the listeners' responses in your presentation. I'll provide more insights in the "C" portion of "P.I.T.C.H."

The major value of these three methods mentioned above is to "get your mirror neurons in line." That is, you are able to truly and deeply increase your confidence by proper and effective preparation.

2. Interview them (if possible)

Here are some valuable moments of your pitch: The moments *before* your pitch!

I advised a client who was going to be one of a line of people pitching to a group of investors to ask these questions if possible: "So what brings you to this event? Is there something you're looking for in particular for a project you'd like to invest in?"

When you have learned a few details prior to your actual pitch, you can increase connection with an investor by addressing the person and their focus-points.

It can sound like this: "Paul, you mentioned that you're looking for a film project that has a greater chance of succeeding because it's in a recognizable genre such as action-thriller or horror."

Be on the lookout for the opportunity to ask a couple questions so that you can tailor your pitch.

3. Target answers to "Worst Questions"

What are the "worst questions" that you do *not* want to answer? Every project has weaknesses. Every leadership team is not perfect. The important plan is to have at least two answers for each "worst question."

The real preparation occurs when you have your coach or someone you trust rehearse with you. That is, the other person asks a Worst Question, and you answer the question.

There's a big difference between writing you answer and actually simulating the pressure-filled moment of your answering a Worst Question.

When I was a new public speaker, I practiced answering the question: "If you're so smart, why ain't you rich?" I had no fear of such a question because I had rehearsed with several people asking me that question on a succession of days.

Here are three examples of Worst Questions:
- How do you have the gall to ask us to fund your current project even though your last company went bankrupt?
- How can you succeed in the clothing industry when

you have no formal training in fashion design?

- You're so young. There's no way you have adequate experience in this industry. How do you think you have a ghost of a chance?

Be sure to practice at least two answers for 10 Worst Questions. You'll have 20 prepared answers. That's useful.

4. Conduct "dialogue"

If you only have 20 minutes to pitch: Talk for 10 minutes and make sure to have a 10-minute conversation with the investors.

You CAN intersperse some "dialogue" in your pitch. Here are examples:

"Just before we began, I had the chance to talk with Sarah. Sarah, you mentioned that an important factor in your decision to invest in a project is XYZ, right? Great. I agree. That's an important component. It's sharp to notice that ..."

You just gave a compliment to Sarah. Good plan! An interesting element of the above comment is that you're doing a valuable action, what author Oren Klaf calls "doling out Alpha Status." What he means is: You are being the "alpha dog" in the room, AND you are showing that you are a peer with the investor. Remember that you're bringing a valuable opportunity to the investors in the room.

5. Help them say "yes"

Years ago, I auditioned for a commercial while the director and two team members assessed my performance. At the end of the audition, I said, "It seems that I'm a match for your commercial. So it looks like we have a *yes* for me to be in your commercial...?" I was nodding my head. The director nodded his head and turned to the person on his left and said, "Um. Yeah, right?"

Still nodding, the director also looked to the other person, who nodded in turn.

That's how I was selected for that commercial. I got my "yes!"

I call this "putting *yes* into the room."

Here's an example of how to end your pitch:

"Because of [Reason #1] and [Reason #2], I encourage you to say yes to funding my project."

I have coached clients to cite two reasons because that gives you two chances to hit one that connects with more investors in the room.

Principle: Making a real connection with investors is more important than merely reciting your pitch in a word-perfect manner.

Countermeasure: Devote extra attention and time to rehearsing important elements of your pitch including your well-prepared answers to Worst Questions.

Power Questions: What are the 10 Worst Questions that investors can ask you? What are you two well-prepared answers for each Worst Question?

Pitch Advantage #4

Secrets So You Pitch and Connect on the Subconscious Level

In one of my recent presentations, I talked of the A.I.M. process of Pitching (**A**lign your mirror neurons; **I**nvite "yes"; and **M**eet them as a peer.)

In the previous section I talked about "mirror neurons" and "get them to say 'yes.'"

Now, we'll focus on how you can effectively *meet investors as a peer.* **You need to rehearse so effectively that you** *prepare your own subconscious mind* **to operate on a higher, more confident level.**

Where will your authentic confidence come from?

First, you connect with the truth that you're bring great value to the table.

Second, you prepare to present well and to answer questions effectively. Then you will convey that you're a leader.

The truth is: **We invest in leaders—not servants.**

One of my mentors said, "You have more power than you think. If they're talking with you, they want something."

Author Oren Klaf tells himself "I am the prize" before he

meets high-level investors or clients. His point is that he is bringing something of great value to the listeners of his pitch.

This is a vital point. Without the innovators/pitch-makers, so much would be missing in this world. You *are* bringing something truly valuable to the table. And in that way, you are a peer of the people in the room.

Lie: People will trust you if you're too deferential (submissive) to them.

Countermeasure: Prepare and rehearse so you meet the person as a peer. Stand forthrightly in the value you bring to the table.

Secret: "My courage always rises at every attempt to intimidate me." – Jane Austen (in her book Pride and Prejudice)

"Don't let what you don't know scare you, because it can become your greatest asset. And if you do things without knowing how they have always been done, you're guaranteed to do them differently." – Sara Blakely, creator of Spanx

When one is too deferential, one shows that one has "lower status." Top investors feel their Alpha Status and they trust others who also have Alpha Status.

The head of an angel investors group told me, "If you go in asking for advice, you get funding. If you go in asking for funding, you'll get advice." I understand her point. Still, it's vital to approach investors as if you're **a colleague asking for a consult.** You do not want to come across as a servant begging for help. Why? We invest in leaders! We do not invest in people who are unsure of their own worth. The reason is: It's takes a confident person to persist, ask the right questions and to pull everyone through the adversity to complete any project.

Principle: Meet them as a peer.

Countermeasure: Rehearse in effective ways so you can present well and effectively answer questions. Focus on the value you bring to the table. Remind yourself that the world needs you to get this project to come to fruition.

Power Question: Are you feeling confident in the value that your project will manifest? What can you do to build up your confidence in your project and your confidence in yourself to bring great value?

Pitch Advantage #5

Think "Brief" and "Give Them a Map"

Cheryl was getting to the end of her pitch. No one's eyes were lit up. In fact, the investors in the room looked somewhat confused.

"Where did I lose them?" she wondered.

Lie: People can follow what you're saying.

Another Lie: Telling the whole, detailed truth is better than "news they can use."

Countermeasures: Use structure. Give people a "map" so they know where they are and what is coming up.

Give them Three Points.

Secret: "Tell the audience what you're going to say, say it; then tell them what you've said." – Dale Carnegie

The best way to talk about "give them a map" is to share an example. **Recently, I was invited to give a speech. Here is the text of the beginning of that speech.**

"I'm standing at the door. In just a couple of moments, I will walk through this door and have a meeting with George Takei—Mr. Sulu of the original *Star Trek*. I'm going to invite him to be in my first feature film.

I'm thinking about what it took for me to get to this point.

And this is the first point of the **three main points** I have for you today: **Express Yourself.**

You'll have *two benefits* with our conversation today:

First, we're talking about how you can persevere.

Second, it's about how you can keep your dream alive!

So **my first main point is: Express Yourself.**

* * *

Above you see the structure that I put into this speech. I included:

- A "grabber" opening of the speech
- Three main points
- Two benefits

At the end of the speech, it works well when you provide:

- A Summary of the Three Main Points
- A "Big Finish"

Here's an example of a big finish to a speech:

"So let me pull it all together for you.

We've talked about what it takes to persevere.

And we've talked about how to keep your dream alive.

So help me out here.

The first one, the beginning of everything is to:

[Audience says, "Express Yourself."]

Number two: If you meet that roadblock, you're going to

[Audience says, "Create a new road."]
And finally, this will lift your life, you
[Audience says, "Say Yes to Yourself."]
Thank you."

A Special Note: For the end of a pitch, you can use this structure:

"Because of [Reason #1] and [Reason #2], I encourage to say yes to funding my project."

Principle: Think "brief" and give them a map.

Countermeasure: Set up an outline for your speech that includes *5 Elements of a Great Speech*
- A "grabber" opening of the speech
- Three main points
- Two benefits
- A Summary of the Three Main Points
- A "Big Finish"

Power Question: How are you going to implement the *5 Elements of a Great Speech* for your next presentation?

Pitch Advantage #6

Answer Tough Questions
(When You Pitch and
When You Deal with the Media)

"Isn't it true that you made big mistakes while you led that company?" the journalist asked Matthew.

"Well ... I ... I didn't—"

"Yes or no. You didn't prepare for the market fluctuations?"

"I—I didn't foresee how the market would shift away from how our product was—I made the mistake in thinking..."

The above interchange turns into a terrible sound bite and even a worse headline in various industry blogs like: "CEO Matthew S__ Admits that He Did Not Prepare for Market Fluctuations ..." Matthew dug himself deeper into the hole with "I made the mistake in thinking..."

Lie: You can wing it when a tough question comes your way.

Countermeasure: Rehearse how you will "catch the question" and convey information that helps your cause. Beware of saying something as a sound bite that hurts your cause.

Secret: "The dumbing down of America is most evident in the slow decay of substantive content in the enormously influential media, the 30 second sound bites (now down to 10 seconds or less) ... a kind of celebration of ignorance." — Carl Sagan

I shared this information in an article (at my blog PitchPowerFest.com):

**Be at Your Best: Pitch Well and
Answer Tough Questions!**

"How did the top filmmakers fail to engage the Silicon Valley investors, Tom?" my friend Jill asked.

"Many of them crashed and burned when they reacted to questions," I replied, noting what I observed at a private investors' meeting in Palo Alto, California.

Here I'm going to share briefly some vital ways to respond (not react) to tough questions.

I have three steps: a) Catch the question, b) Answer the question and c) Shine light on the Diamond.

1. Catch the Question

As I work with clients, I've seen many of them recoil and step backwards when they're asked a tough question. Wrong move. Stepping backwards shows that you're unsure of the value you bring.

Instead, over the years, I have conditioned myself to step two steps forward when someone asks a question.

I invite you to step toward the person and say something like this (to "catch the question"):

- "Susan, I'm glad you brought that up. I was going to address that in the next segment. Let's do this now."
- "George, I can see that's important to you."

When you answer a question in that above manner, you show that you are *not* uneasy about the question. You also give yourself time to think. I call it "thinkspace."

2. Answer the Question and Shine Light on the Diamond

When you answer a question, you do NOT have to accept the premise.

Picture this:

George (potential investor) asks, with an edge: "Anita, how do you have the gall to ask us for money when your first company went belly up?"

Anita replies: "George, I can see that means a lot to you. I learned a lot from the experience with the previous company. Recently, while working as vice president of XYZ Company, I've learned of a market segment that no one was aware of three years ago. I have the focus and the data to back up that this is a prime opportunity for investors like you to take advantage of some new data and new technology."

The above answer covers something that is implied by George's tough question: The possibility that Anita is incompetent.

Anita does *not* reply in any way in which she could hurt her own cause. She will NOT provide some self-conscious, self-denigrating comment that could be recorded as a terrible sound bite that issued from her own mouth.

Instead, she expresses "the Diamond"—also known as "talking points"—that she is competent (working as vice president at XYZ Company) and that she sees new opportunities (backed up by new data and new technology).

The truth is: With great coaching and proper rehearsal, you can prepare for the *10 Worst Questions You Don't Want to Answer.*

When you do that, you'll be so prepared, that you will know, even in your subconscious mind, that you have real value to convey to potential investors.

That's when you're strong and ready ... and you will succeed.

* * * * * *

Dealing with the Media and the Sound Bite Emphasis

"The bias of the mainstream media is toward sensationalism, conflict, and laziness." – Jon Stewart

Above I mentioned: "She will NOT provide some self-conscious, self-denigrating comment that could be recorded as a terrible sound bite that issued from her own mouth."

Be careful to avoid "accepting the premise."

You can answer a question in a way that emphasizes what helps your cause.

As I noted above, this quote from Anita contains no self-condemnation:

"George, I can see that means a lot to you. I learned a lot from the experience with the previous company. Recently, while working as vice president of XYZ Company, I've learned of a market segment that no one was aware of three years ago. I have the focus and the data to back up that this is a prime opportunity for investors like you to take advantage of some new data and new technology."

Rehearsal is key. Practice answering the tough questions. There is no substitute.

Principle: It's necessary to actually practice receiving tough questions and then using ways to "catch the question."

Countermeasure: Rehearse effectively. Practice the methods of "catch the question" and "answer the question and shine light on the diamond."

Power Questions: What are six ways you can "catch the question"? Do these ways feel natural as you say them out loud? When will you practice with a coach or trusted advisor in how you respond to tough questions?

Special Note: If you're asked a tough question, you can use a phrase to give yourself some moments to think about it. You could say something like: *"I'll need to pause for a moment. I want my reply to be valuable to you."*

When you make such a statement in a mild tone of voice, you demonstrate that you are *not* thrown off by the question. You demonstrate poise and confidence.

Tom Marcoux

Pitch Advantage #7

Prepare a Compelling Story that Moves Emotions

"I want to develop a Ted Talk that goes viral," said Nick, one of my clients.

"Let's start with your primary, target market," I said.

"Women 38-60 years old."

In the rest of the conversation, I brought up these questions:

- What are their fears?
- What do they find funny?
- What do they find charming?
- How will you fascinate them with the title of your talk?
- What will make you both credible and charming in the first few seconds of your talk?
- How do you end the talk so they want to applaud and immediately forward your Ted Talk to their five closest friends?

This is all about strategy.

Now let's look at *7 Structure Elements that make a story*

compelling:
1. Problem
2. Villain or significant antagonist (opposition)
3. It looks impossible to solve.
4. Things are tried
5. Tension.
6. Suspense.
7. Hero (or hero with team) barely succeed.

Lie: You'll convince people through the laser-focus on facts.

Countermeasure: Prepare a compelling story that moves emotions.

Secret: "People still love a good story, and I don't think that will change." – Bob Iger, CEO of The Walt Disney Company

When I connected with author Joe Vitale, he emphasized that the value of a story is that it does not bring up resistance. "It gets under the radar," Joe said.

When you proclaim a fact, a significant number of people will immediately resist. A well-crafted story will avoid such resistance.

It's valuable to seize attention with a great story *and* to back it up with relevant facts as needed.

The classic phrase is: *Facts just tell. Stories sell.*

Principle: Facts just tell. Stories sell.

Countermeasure: Craft a story that compels attention *and* avoids inciting resistance in the listener.

Power Question: What is most important to your listener? How can you craft a story that focuses on what he or she cares about most?

Book 3:
Success Advantages

Success Advantage #1

Think "Brand" Every day

At Walt Disney World, the attraction attendant said, "I'm sorry. You can't bring that ice cream cone on the ride." The little girl burst into tears. Her parents' faces dropped into concerned frowns.

The attendant said, "I'll hold your cone for you."

The girl's face brightened in a smile.

After the girl returned from the ride, the attendant handed her an ice cream cone.

Here's the twist: The parents knew that in the hot Florida weather, the original ice cream cone would have melted into a puddle.

What had happened? The attendant ordered a new ice cream cone so the girl would be delighted upon her return from the ride.

Now, *that* **is a story celebrating the Walt Disney World brand!** What do we get from this story? Disney "cast members" (employees) often put in extra effort to create a delighted customer experience.

Lie: Building your brand is a sometime thing.

Countermeasure: Focus on ways to create a terrific emotional relationship for your customer *with* your brand.

Secret: "It's a good time to be in the content business though, the branded content business." – Bob Iger, CEO of The Walt Disney Company

I admit it. I am a great customer for the collection of brands that The Walt Disney Company provides.

I visit Disney Theme Parks. I watch films under the brands of Marvel Studios, Lucasfilm, Pixar and Walt Disney Animation.

Above Bob Iger emphasized "the branded content business."

So let's look closely at building brands.

Before, I go further, I'll share a few words on **your personal brand.** It's the answer to the question, *What are you best known for?* It's also the answer to: *What five words come to mind when someone mentions your name in conversation?*

I've coached clients to have these elements: trustworthy, helpful, organized and respectful (that one can remember with "T.H.O.R.").

Now, let's continue with elements of business brands.

We'll use the B.R.A.N.D. process:

B – build an emotional relationship

R – realize your digital footprint

A – account for things

N – nurture authenticity

D – deliver something special

1. Build an emotional relationship

"Great companies that build an enduring brand have an emotional relationship with customers that has no barrier. And that emotional relationship is based on the most important characteristic, which is trust." – Howard Schultz, CEO of Starbucks

Howard Schultz alerts us to what creates massive customer loyalty. It's the *emotional experience* the customer has. Make sure that your customer is so pleased he or she returns again and again.

"Do what you do so well that they will want to see it again and bring their friends." – Walt Disney

I am adding an additional component: **Identity. Who does your customer want to be?** The person who buys the latest iPhone likely has a different self-definition than one who buys a Droid cell phone.

Certain books point out that motorcyclists that purchase a Harley-Davidson motorcycle often are part of a certain culture.

Jimmy Buffett parlayed his success with a song "Margaritaville" into a series of cafes and even 30 Cheeseburger in Paradise restaurants. The song inspired a feeling and even an "identity."

2. Realize your digital footprint

"Social media is changing the way we communicate and the way we are perceived, both positively and negatively. Every time

you post a photo, or update your status, you are contributing to your own digital footprint and personal brand." – Amy Jo Martin

How is your company perceived on social media? At one point, a number of companies received a lot of flak when they tried to post humorous tweets based on current events. These tweets backfired.

Pay close attention to how your company's social media presence builds your brand or tears it down.

Start with the question: "What is *most important* for people to know about their experience with what we offer?"

3. Account for things

"The keys to brand success are self-definition, transparency, authenticity and accountability." – Simon Mainwaring

What a company counts demonstrates what they value.

If your company only counts how many sales are made and does not take into account the experiences that the customers are having, then something is *off*.

On the other hand, Disney's internal newsletter publication "Eyes and Ears" features "Magical Moments" which occur when a Disney cast member creates a special experience for a guest (like the experience the little girl had when her ice cream cone was waiting for her).

At Disney Parks, Disney cast members approach the guests (customers) as they leave for the evening. They ask about how the person's day went. Disney pays close attention to how people rate their experiences.

4. Nurture authenticity

"Brand is just a perception, and perception will match reality over time. Sometimes it will be ahead, other times it will be behind. But brand is simply a collective impression some have about a

product." – Elon Musk

Brand may be perception, but how can we make that perception good for our cause?

Be authentic. Stand for something like quality and creating delighted customers.

Twenty-one years later, I still remember when a Franklin-Covey company representative made up for an error in shipping. He asked me, "How can I make this better?" I replied, "You could send me ..." And I named a couple of products.

I was impressed that the Franklin-Covey company empowered its representative to make amends for a problem.

Be sure that your team members back up the claims to take good care of customers with appropriate action.

5. Deliver something special

"Your premium brand had better be delivering something special, or it's not going to get the business." – Warren Buffett

Years ago, I wrote about "customer delight—that's when you provide something extra and surprising."

I began this section with the story of a Disney cast member getting another ice cream cone to delight the little girl and her parents.

Delivering something special involves training your team members to be on the lookout for opportunities to exceed customers' expectations.

Just a moment ago, I looked up at a corkboard here in my office. I saw a row of Disney pins that I have collected from multiple Disney Parks visits.

Disney is doing something right!

Principle: Building and maintaining your brand calls for exceptional attention to detail.

Countermeasure: Make sure that you train your team members to stay alert for opportunities to exceed customers' expectations.

Power Question: What do your customers expect? What would be extra and surprising for them? How can you make sure that they have a positive emotional relationship with your brand and company?

Success Advantage #2

Build a Buffer—Get Stronger

Years ago, author Roger Mellot talked about a man confronted with three huge life stresses: his teenage daughter was pregnant, his wife wanted a divorce and he needed heart bypass surgery.

Roger asked his audience, "What should he do?"

Some audience members hesitated. They were baffled.

"Bypass!" Roger said.

Many of us have accomplished a lot. We've faced tough odds and difficulties.

There is something to pay attention to: Something tough is coming. Maybe it's a health problem or the need to lay off employees. Something is coming.

So the vital thing is to focus on our health: body, mind and spirit. That's in line with "get the bypass surgery."

Lie: You're as strong as you need to be.

Countermeasure: Build a buffer.

Secret: "Build a superreserve in every area: have more than enough." – Thomas Leonard

As a leader in business and your own life, you'll be called to stretch and endure as you've never have before. That is the challenge and that is the adventure.

Still, too many of us are living on the edge of burnout or disaster.

With one of my clients, I noted, "Picture a ruler. You're at point A. Let's say at one inch on this ruler. Perhaps, you'll stretch to point D. And that's four inches outward. It can be helpful to pull back to point C. Between C and D—that's your buffer. You'll make sure to have a reserve of energy, sleep and more so your capacity can handle the surprise problem or even the surprise disaster."

Thomas Leonard suggested that we have a superreserve in all areas. What does that look like?

If you can get by on five hours of sleep, how do you feel on seven hours of sleep?

If you can get by on taking a walk three times a week, how strong are you when you get in a walk every day?

If you think your relationship is okay with your spouse, how strong would your relationship be if you included a date night and even a couple's therapy session every two weeks?

People who live on the edge tend to fall off at times.

Pull back from the edge. Put in a buffer of energy and time.

Author Cheryl Richardson made the point that taking care of yourself is not just about adding something to your life. It's about cutting what does not fit.

With one of my clients, I suggested, "Let's look at this topic. *Eliminate critical life-killing elements.*"

What in your life is draining your energy?

We tell ourselves stories. Some stories are life-building.

Others are life-draining.

Make good choices.

Principle: Back away from the edge and put in a buffer.

Countermeasure: See how you can develop superreserves in terms of sleep, exercise, nutrition, personal finances and more.

Power Question: Do you have any superreserves? Where can your life break down? How can you build up a buffer in your life?

Tom Marcoux

Success Advantage #3

Overpower Procrastination

"I just can't seem to get over this procrastination block that's holding me back," my client Edward said.

"Procrastination tends to arise from two things: You don't know how to do something or you're anticipating pain. It's time to use strategy instead of falling back on some notion that you're supposed to just tough it out. As if that's heroic or something," I replied.

Lie: To overcome procrastination, you need to kick yourself forward and use "discipline" every time.

Countermeasure: You need strategy so you don't fall back on trying to us "willpower."

Secret: "When someone mentions procrastination, they're saying 'I can't do this with my own resources.'"

– Thomas Leonard

I've written a lot about overcoming procrastination. In fact, a major section of my online course "Soar with Confidence" is devoted to practical methods so one can be free of procrastination.

In my book, *Soar! Nothing Can Stop You* I share **12 Elements of the Compelling** to help the reader become stronger than procrastination.

Here I will emphasize a process inspired by Thomas Leonard's comment "I can't do this with my own resources."

This leads us to clear next step: Apply more resources. How?

a) Add something to the mix

If doing a certain form of paperwork is boring or painful, add music of your choice. Perhaps, make phone calls from your balcony to enjoy the cool breeze.

b) Add a person to the mix

On those occasions in which I hired an assistant on a particular project, I saw my productivity rise. I got things ready before the appointed hour. Then during the session while the assistant was helping, I moved very quickly, making a series of decisions. Why? I wanted my investment in the fee to yield a lot of benefits.

c) Add training or new knowledge

If you keep doing things in your current patterns, you're likely to stay stuck. For example, I procrastinated on meditating because I simply found it uncomfortable to sit still for a long time.

I did some research and found out that I could add a certain form of meditating (including making the sound of "Ahhhhh") for 3 minutes per morning.

My daily life improved when I added this new pattern to my life.

From research connected to Stanford University, I learned that our willpower is strongest in the morning, so I eat salad for breakfast. Now, this is something I do automatically. No procrastination.

Principle: Use strategy to break patterns of procrastination.

Countermeasure: Observe your behavior, then add resources (including, perhaps, a person or training/new knowledge).

Power Question: What are your patterns of procrastination? How can you use strategy to break patterns of procrastination?

Success Advantage #4

Test in Your Marketing Processes.
Ask Customers.

On a number of occasions, I've written an article and seen good responses at LinkedIn, Facebook and Twitter. I then was inspired to expand the article into a book. (I've written 41 books so far.)

My article served as a test. I'm testing titles and ideas to see if they stick.

At one point, I was writing a book and was thinking to call it *Get Real or Get Hurt.*

During a particular workshop, I was talking about testing product names, and I was inspired to try a couple of titles with the attendees.

Only one person voted for *Get Real or Get Hurt.* Everyone else voted for *What Rich People Don't Say About Getting Rich* (which is now the title of one of my books on Amazon.com).

Lie: You can go on your gut feelings for a marketing campaign.

Countermeasure: Test in your marketing processes. Ask customers.

Secret: "We see our customers as invited guests to a party, and we are the hosts. It's our job every day to make every important aspect of the customer experience a little bit better." – Jeff Bezos, founder of Amazon.com

A couple of the books that I've written do not gain buyers each month. At the time I wrote the book, my impression was that I was onto an idea that would be attractive. Oh, well.

I've observed that we do **not** know how something will work until we put it into the marketplace.

Still, we need to realize that a good idea may just have arrived in the marketplace at the wrong time.

For example, for eight years, author John Gray addressed audiences and talked about the differences between men and women and what causes havoc with their romantic relationships with each other.

He was on the receiving end of some angry responses. He said that, at the time, people were more interested in talking about equality between the genders.

Then after about eight years, he wrote and published a book *Men Are from Mars, Women Are from Venus.* This book proved to be a huge bestseller. Did he have prior difficulties because the American society was not yet interested in hearing his ideas? Or was springboard the catchy banner of *Men Are from Mars, Women Are from Venus?*

The point we get from this is: Keep trying different combinations. Test your ideas, and see what happens in the marketplace.

Principle: Testing is vital because our gut feelings might not line up with the realities in the marketplace.

Countermeasure: Test at a number of phases during your project. [The example was publishing an article and seeing responses on LinkedIn, Facebook and Twitter.]

Power Question: How are you testing your ideas with real potential customers?

Tom Marcoux

Success Advantage #5

Shift Your Thoughts

When I met Wayne Dyer (some time ago), I was wearing a tie. Wayne said in a cheerful voice, "Hello, sir!" How fun! That became my "hello, sir" tie. I said, "Could I give you a hug?" I'm glad I got a chance to thank Wayne by giving him a hug. Some time ago, upon hearing of Wayne's death, I ordered his book *I Can See Clearly Now*—I wasn't ready to let him go. So I read a portion of his book each day. I also wrote about his wise words in my blog article "Celebrate Wayne Dyer's Life—and Express YOUR Light."

Lie: Just a few words will not give you a new perception.

Countermeasure: Be active in your own search for new ideas to shift your perspective.

Secret: "There is no way to happiness, happiness is the way."

– Dr. Wayne Dyer

In these days [when I wrote this section], since Wayne Dyer passed away, I'm thinking about brief, life-enhancing quotes he gave us. Let's see how these three pithy quotes inspire our empowering patterns of thought now.

1. "There is no way to happiness, happiness is the way." – Wayne Dyer

How much ice cream will make you happy? How many new cars?

People who get caught up in the "hamster treadmill" of trying to go directly to happiness through more toys, more food and more experiences may find themselves greatly disappointed.

If that's true, then where is happiness? Happiness is in this moment—doing what you are now doing.

There are plenty of ways to get caught up in what makes us miserable. One pervasive way is to get stuck in worrying.

"Replace worry with action." – Steve Chandler

So I invite you to use this empowering pattern. When a worrisome thought arises, think "Stop—Replace."

I've found this to be helpful because in running my own company, I've had moments of serious worry. Then I remember "Replace worry with action."

Other times, I have a thought, "Oh! I have so much to do."

Then I tell myself: "STOP." And I replace the thought with

"I am doing this one thing in this one moment. I'll do the next thing after this one thing."

So in the spirit of Wayne's comment "There is no way to happiness, happiness is the way":

Seek to make the way you're living moment to moment into a "happy path." You deep breathe. You connect with feeling gratitude for the blessings you do have in this moment.

2. **"If you change the way you look at things, the things you look at change." – Wayne Dyer**

Think of the reflexive way we look at things:

- "That will make me happy."
- "That's going to hurt."
- "You're wrong. And you hurt me."

Certainly, we do not look at everything as if it will hurt us. Still, we spend a lot of time judging people and things.

Think about it. Are you using your brain in a skillful manner?

Every time a worrisome thought arises, do you obsess over it?

Wayne's comment: "If you change the way you look at things, the things you look at change" inspires us to find new, empowering ways to interpret our life situation.

When a pain-inducing thought arises, consider these new ways to look at your current situation:

- What can I learn here?
- What lesson would Higher Power have me learn so I can make my life better and better?

3. **"There is no scarcity of opportunity to make a living at what you love; there's only scarcity of resolve to make it happen." – Wayne Dyer**

Some people will hold onto the idea that Wayne Dyer was just one of the "lucky ones."

But let's remember, he faced a big risk earlier in life. Wayne left his tenured teaching position at St. John's University in New York to pursue his destiny as both speaker and author. Yes—it worked for him.

This statement "There is no scarcity of opportunity to make a living at what you love; there's only scarcity of resolve to make it happen" is a big challenge to many of us.

Really?—you can make a living at what you love?

I have an answer to this question. I say, "Let's find out!"

At different times in my life, I've made a living doing what felt personally meaningful to me. I've earned income as a graduate school instructor, as a model/actor (years ago), as a speaker, and as an author. Now, I do a lot of work as an Executive Coach and Spoken Word Strategist.

Are there times when we need to do both a "rent job" and our "dream job"—simultaneously? Yes—I've seen that to be true. Many years ago, I worked at a bank for 8 hours a day and then raced home to edit a feature film for several hours—every day! Thank goodness, I had a great friend to help me edit the feature film.

If you love writing poetry, perhaps, you may not make a living at it. Still, let's look again at Wayne's phrase: "There is no scarcity of opportunity." For some poets, they might find an opportunity to earn income by setting their poetry to music—in song writing.

I'll emphasize that Wayne invites us to have the resolve to make it happen. Will it be your destiny to make a large income at what you love doing? Who knows?

Still, what we can know is: You will not find out unless you resolve to persist and keep taking effective action.

Wayne said, **"You can never get enough of what you don't want."**

I've seen people get stuck in "golden shackles." They do a job they hate and then give themselves the salve of big, expensive vacations. They say, "I deserve this."

Wayne's comment, "You can never get enough of what you don't want" relates to how you can NOT fill the hole of a job you hate with enough vacations or toys (cars, etc.).

Wayne said that when he was drinking to excess that he could never get enough alcohol-laden drinks. Because he did

NOT want the alcohol.

He wanted a better life.

I invite you to reflect on Wayne's above quotes and see how you might step up your actions for your own better life.

Principle: An idea can shift your perception and empower you to feel better and to get more done.

Countermeasure: Pick a series of ideas to memorize and recall when you need to empower yourself in the moment.

Power Question: Do you have a few favorite quotes that put your thinking on an empowered track?

Success Advantage #6

Use a Solid and Flexible Stance

About 30 years ago, my father told me of a film in which a character, a mailman said, "I'm a mailman. No. That's what I *do.* That's *not* **who I am.**"

Who are you?

How do you measure yourself?

Do you only focus on your professional achievements?

I've interviewed successful people who look like a success to the outside world, but they let slip how inside they're a wreck.

Sustainable Success is built on a solid and flexible stance.

For a number of years, I was trained in karate moves. I learned to have a stance that was both solid and flexible. You needed to be solid so you jump forward and punch or kick.

Furthermore, if one stood flatfooted, an opponent would sweep one's forward foot, sending one tumbling down.

You, as a leader, cannot afford to be off balance.

So we'll focus on helping you strengthen yourself in your "total life."

Lie: Relying on "business strengths" is enough to make you a great leader.

Countermeasure: Develop a Solid and Flexible Stance.

Secret: "With every experience, you alone are painting your own canvas, thought by thought, choice by choice."
– Oprah Winfrey

1. Lie: Relying on "business strengths" is enough to make you a great leader.

By this point in life, you know your strengths. If you were talking with me in a coaching session you might say:

- I'm good with forecasting
- I'm a good speaker
- I'm good at keeping the momentum going

The next question is: Are you strong, stable and calm?

Why would this be important? Because people tend to trust those who are calm in the storm.

To be that calm in the storm, you need a solid foundation as a human being.

2. Countermeasure and how this section's Secret has a role in improving your life.

To have a Solid and Flexible Stance, you need a good foundation in the rest of your life.

How do you do that?

You take care of the real business of living a strong life. You face the realities of living on an extraordinary path.

Oprah said, *"With every experience, you alone are painting your own canvas, thought by thought, choice by choice."*

I invite you to consider your choices related to your WHOLE life. Many of us are making good choices for business, but we're allowing ourselves (body, mind and soul) to teeter on the edge of burnout and disaster.

We'll now pay close attention by focusing on *The Top Five Regrets of the Dying* by author Bronnie Ware.

1. I wish I'd had the courage to live a life true to myself, not the life others expected of me.
2. I wish I hadn't worked so hard.
3. I wish I'd had the courage to express my feelings.
4. I wish I had stayed in touch with my friends.
5. I wish that I had let myself be happier.

Special Note: This section addresses two vital things: free-floating anxiety and "free-floating emptiness."

Free-floating anxiety is defined as "a vague, uneasy feeling of discomfort or dread, accompanied by an autonomic response (the source often nonspecific or unknown to the individual); a feeling of apprehension caused by anticipation of danger." (thefreedictionary.com)

"Free-floating emptiness" is a term I've coined to refer to a vague, uneasy feeling of discomfort, restlessness and sadness. The person may have the outside signs of success and happiness (large income, big house, family, friends) but the person feels on the edge of burnout.

For both the anxiety and emptiness that I describe above, the focus point is "vague." I invite you, if you feel some version of anxiety and emptiness, to avoid "letting it be." It's better to face the reality of your discomfort. And the below ideas and methods can be helpful. (Also, you might consider working with a mental health professional.)

Now, I'll share a few ideas related to the *Five Regrets:*

1. I wish I'd had the courage to live a life true to myself, not the life others expected of me.

Many of us find ourselves living in some kind of "box." Sure, your current box may have gold-trimmings—or not.

I work with several clients who are extremely goal-oriented. Goals can be helpful. Still, you can get all the big goals done and feel empty.

Whose goals are you fulfilling, anyway?

My clients have found it helpful to divide goals into these categories:

Golden Pull Goals – These are goals that are "shiny"—they pull you forward to a better future.

Dark Boot Goals – These are goals concerned with avoiding pain (the dark boot hitting one in the rear).

Green Tranquility Goals – These are focus points/activities that one does *to strengthen one's being.* Some examples include: daily quiet time/meditation, exercise, good nutrition and enough renewing sleep.

I've learned that only having a "future-focus" with Golden Pull Goals can get one to experience life way out of balance. If you have no time for Green Tranquility Goals and daily peace and happiness, you're living in an unstainable way. Instead, focus on doing that which strengthens you.

Now it's your turn. What will you add or subtract from your daily life so you're sure that you living a life true to yourself?

2. I wish I hadn't worked so hard.

Does "working hard" mean "too many hours at work and too few hours with family"?

Does it mean working at a job that does not connect with your true talents and interests? If you hate your daily work-life, you *are* working too hard.

Here's another point: Is working to hard referring to one giving all of one's energy at the office and just having a few dregs for family members?

Author Sheryl Sandberg (COO of Facebook) wrote about *leaving the office at 5:30 pm* and having dinner with her children and husband (who later passed away at 47 years old).

Now it's your turn. What is our self-assessment about your own work? Do you say (even just to yourself) that you're working too hard? Do you want to adjust your schedule so you make more time and space for what means the most to you?

3. I wish I'd had the courage to express my feelings.

Some of us do not express certain feelings because we do not want to rock the boat—perhaps, at home.

Some of us run from our home life and find refuge at work where we're in our element. Years ago, author and speaker Roger Mellot talked about how, if you take a test pilot and stick him in a day care center, he might just fall apart.

What's the solution? First, realize that you might need help. We may be good at something but *training is required* to be good at something else.

A test pilot gets trained. Why? Because when people are under stress they fall back on their training.

It may seem strange, but a test pilot might need some form of training to "survive" a day at home with the kids.

It's good to practice—yes, even rehearse—how you effectively share your feelings.

The classic way is to use "I" statements. For example, one could say, "This is not working for me. When I'm talking about my day, I just want to vent for a while. So please hold off on the suggestions. Until I ask for a comment. When you just listen, then I feel loved."

Often, we regret missing opportunities to expressing our love to our loved ones.

It helps to practice (and then later tell the loved one):

"You did a great job doing _____. I really appreciate it."

"You're important to me. I love you."

"I care about you. Okay, I'm upset at the moment. I expect I'll be forgiving you … when I can."

[**Special Note:** This last example may feel strange to a number of people. But imagine if you had someone who *still cares about you* even when they're upset.]

Now it's your turn. What feelings have you been holding back? Do you need to practice saying things related to your feelings in non-threatening ways? How will you get help? Will you work with a coach or therapist?

4. I wish I had stayed in touch with my friends.

How often do you see friends who are important to you?

When it comes to friendships, I'm in favor of being selective.

After years of experience, I've learned:

Some friendships are novels.

Some friendships are short stories.

Some friendships are a sentence. Put a period on that and get away!

My point here is **consider devoting more time with those certain friends who lift you up and do NOT drain your energy.**

Now it's your turn. Which friends actually support you and lift your mood? Will you get your calendar out and call some friends and set up get-togethers now?

5. I wish that I had let myself be happier.

The topic of happiness is a deep one and in some ways, it's a complex area to focus on.

Let's begin. We can break down "let myself be happier" into:

a) Devoted energy and time to those parts of life that bring me happiness

b) Shift my daily habits so I can have happy moments often

a) Devoted energy and time to those parts of life that bring me happiness

Some people put their own happiness as last on the list. So what happens? Nothing. They do not get around to having happy moments.

A couple of times, I've asked certain clients: "Are you numb?" Numb is close to "death." It's certainly **not** "feeling fully alive."

Sometimes, it's true that going directly for happiness does not work.

"Happiness is not a goal...it's a by-product of a life well lived." - *Eleanor Roosevelt*

Still, **we can be kind to ourselves.** Consider treating yourself like you are your own best friend. Some actions do lead to more peace and enjoyment.

What works for you? Listening to good music? Having a good run? Assembling a puzzle with a child (family member)?

Now it's your turn. What are some things can you do on a daily basis to give yourself access to good experiences and happy moments?

b) Shift my daily habits so I can have happy moments more often

What does it take for you to enjoy a happy moment? If your reflex is to say something like "I'll be happy when our client Kervin is _____," then you have a problem. Why? Because you seem to postpone happiness.

A number of people have found it quite helpful to learn to have a happy moment with "little things."

I have a habit of saying, "I'm grateful for every blessing."

Furthermore, I learned a method from author Chade-Meng Tan. He said, "You decided to attend this workshop. You got into your car and now you're here. Did you say, 'I'm so happy!'"?

So the idea is to take a moment and say something like: "I wanted to read this book. I'm reading it. I'M SO HAPPY!"

(I admit it. Just saying that silly thing gets me to smile and sometimes even laugh!)

Now it's your turn. What will you do to make space to enjoy little moments each day?

* * * * * *

Let's face the truth. We're not standing still. We're either getting stronger and better—or we're starting to drift away from healthy living.

You CAN design your life as one of success and happiness.

Principle: Reduce free floating anxiety and free floating emptiness by devoting conscious effort to eliminate the *Top Five Regrets of the Dying*.

Countermeasure: Review the *Top Five Regrets of the Dying* and do what is necessary to enjoy those things in life that make you a stronger, more fulfilled human being.

Power Question: Which of the *Top Five Regrets of the Dying* grabbed your heart? What bothered you? What will you do to, perhaps, streamline your schedule so you have the energy and time for that which is important to your life?

Tom Marcoux

Bonus Material:

1) Want to Become Lucky?
Learn About "Smart Lucky"

"I need some better luck!" Terry, a friend, said.

I listened for a time, and then I said, "Would you like me to share with you a useful idea of how to improve your luck?"

"Yes!" Terry replied.

Learn about "Smart Lucky"

Do you have the ability to turn things around?

Do you call yourself lucky?

A number of researchers have noted that people who call themselves lucky, who believe themselves to be lucky, actually have more positive experiences! It's a positive self-fulfilling prophecy.

Why? **Maybe because their mindset is looking to make things better.** Perhaps, they can better see how to turn things around. They can turn something disappointing into an opportunity for something better.

Recently, I was asked by a journalist to share some lucky things in my own life:

I replied with this:

"Here's my film industry lucky journey. I write a screenplay, and I'm in Silicon Valley. My screenplay is passed from one software engineer to another software engineer to a real estate developer to the California Motion Picture Commissioner. This Commissioner gets me—for free—an American Eagle airplane and the San Luis Obispo Airport to use for the big finish of my feature film. I direct/write/co-produce this feature film that goes to the Cannes Film market and gains international distribution.

"A short time before filming the big action scene at San Luis Obispo Airport, I had a meeting with George Takei ("Mr. Sulu" of *Star Trek*) who said that he was too old for the leading role. So my co-producer turns to me and says, 'Tom, you play the role.' I then turn into an actor-stuntman [The article for *Psychology Today* included a photo of me as a stuntman landing a jet ski in the flatbed of a moving pickup truck.]

"Then I get the chance to direct a second feature film. On the set, the father of a young actor tells me about a film group. I see their website, and this leads to my being a graduate school / college level instructor … even training MBA students at Stanford University."

"You can't connect the dots looking forward; you can only connect them looking backwards. So you have to trust that the dots will somehow connect in your future." – Steve Jobs

Here's What I Call "Smart Lucky"

Just before my film industry journey began, I was offered a $20,000 budget for my band to make a music album. (This was some years ago.)

Some days later, I got a clear, intuitive feeling to end this project. Something was off.

Because I closed the chapter of making this music album, I was subsequently free to begin my film industry journey.

Some people might call the music album not working out as bad luck.

To me, listening to my intuition was "smart." And this is part of what I call "Smart Lucky."

Now it's your turn. When have you experienced the closing of one door and the opening to a new door of opportunity? What situation has recently disappointed you? How can you take effective action and make things better?

I call this: *Make Victory Blossom from Ashes of Disappointment.*

This is the truth: If you adopt a proactive mindset, you can open the door for more lucky opportunities.

Principle: "Smart Lucky" is the ability to turn around what on the surface appears like an unlucky occurrence.

Power Questions: How can you turn around a result that disappoints you? Who can you talk with to get new and better ideas?

Bonus Material #2

Use Your Real Power so You Succeed

"What's one thing I need so I become truly successful?" my new client Adam asked.

"You need to be skillful about handling fear," I replied.

Over years of running companies, I've learned that fear arises every week. That is, if you're doing your job correctly in making things happen. You're supposed to be stretching and growing. You're supposed to be doing things you've never done before.

As an Executive Coach and the Spoken Word Strategist, I've said to clients: "How can you do anything fresh if you don't do something different?"

Picture this. **You'll do better if you can reliably shift your perspective on purpose.**

Think of your personal perspective as a zoom-lens.

The zoom-lens has multiple settings.

All of us are familiar with "zooming in" which brings something far away, closer to us.

Another setting is "zoomed out to wide angle"—that is, when we can see a wider expanse.

1. Let's begin with "Zooming in."

You can think of an overall vision for the future, and that's zooming in. As a feature film director, I know that the zoom lens pulls a picture toward you.

2. Change to "Zoomed Out."

You also need to see the whole picture—that's the zoom-lens in the "zoomed-out" mode, giving you the vision of a wide-angle lens.

3. Focus on something close to you now.

Once, I guided a particular client as I said, "You're zooming-in on the horizon. But your shoe is untied. So turn the 'camera' of your consciousness to your shoe. Take care of what is right here and right now."

We begin to do better in life by using this question: What is the best use of your effort and time in this moment NOW?

If you're stuck in fear, you're probably focused on something dis-empowering.

Shift your perspective. Zoom-in on your overall vision (that is, bring the picture of the bright future close to you.).

The second step is crucial. Change your focus to this present moment.

Ask yourself this empowering question: What is the best use of my effort and time in this moment NOW?

I've worked with clients who have a big, compelling goal to work on. Still, they can sometimes feel overwhelmed by the magnitude of that big dream. It's understandable that the goal feels "So Big!" — and that it is overwhelming.

Here's what you can do.

Shift your focus to the present moment. What is one small thing that you can do to move in a positive forward direction?

My clients have said that they can do these small actions:

- Rehearse before making a vital phone call
- Write up two "if-then alternatives" so they're ready for certain objections their customer is likely to raise
- Take a 10-minute walk at lunch time to refresh themselves to be productive in the afternoon

You handle fear by training yourself to shift your focus point so you can be productive.

Now it's your turn. What can you do in the next 10 minutes that will help you make some incremental progress?

Shift your focus and manifest the life you truly want.

Principle: Change your focus to the present moment.

Power Question: What can you do in the present moment that will take you forward in a positive direction?

Tom Marcoux

Bonus Material #3:

Are You Addicted? How You Can Rise to Real Success

My client, Mary, described her pattern after work of watching more and more TV shows and losing sleep. I asked her: "Are you addicted?"

What is one sign of addiction? You need more and more of something for it to give you a "high" or at least to help you feel "okay." Here's another sign: the behavior is working for you less and less.

We're talking about this in the context of "Be Heard and Be Trusted." If you get to the point that you cannot trust yourself, you will radiate an energy of "untrustworthy." So it's really valuable to confront the necessary questions and even to get help if necessary.

Another question that comes up is: "What pain are you trying to numb so you do not have to feel it?"

Consider: Are you in distress? Are you overwhelmed? Or stressed out—or even burned out?

Questions like those above may be the tip of the iceberg. A number of us may find it helpful to work with a therapist.

As an Executive Coach, I have some clients who work with me *and* a therapist.

This reminds me of a dentist who saved my sweetheart's life. How? He noticed that she had certain discoloration in her mouth. It turned out that she had Idiopathic thrombocytopenic purpura. So a dentist referred my sweetheart (his client) to a medical doctor.

Similarly, an Executive Coach can refer a client to seek a

consultation with a mental health professional.

My point here is: It's valuable to observe your behavior and see what may be an area of concern.

Here's another sign of addiction: You're doing so much of the addiction-related behavior that the rest of your life is going upside down. I've even noticed this concern for myself. I like to write. Still, I make sure to get my other work done so that writing does NOT take over my life.

In this section, we're not going to be able to cover the deep details of extreme addiction.

For now, let's talk about something mild.

If you find that you're leaning toward addiction-like behavior, observe whether you're becoming rigid in your behavior-pattern.

If you get extremely frustrated that you cannot do your set pattern, you might be in the middle of some form of addiction.

Certainly, we realize that addiction to drugs (including alcohol) can devastate a life. A serious intervention may be necessary.

In closing, I'm acting as your Executive Coach in that I'm bringing up something that may be impacting your ability to rise higher and higher in success and happiness.

The truth is: It's often best to *keep a log of your behavior.* Why? **Because without a log, we only have a vague idea. Such an idea may not reflect the reality of your situation.**

I'll give another example. I keep a log of my sleep because I then can make sure to get more sleep if I have too few hours on a particular night.

From interviews with successful people, I've observed that people who create sustainable success have a full support system. Additionally, they face reality and take action to pull themselves together if they "drift" away from healthy living.

Take great care of yourself.

Make sure that you stay strong, and you release yourself from any chains!

Principle: Keep a log of your behavior so you can see the reality of your situation.

Power Question: How can you log your behavior so you can make incremental progress?

Tom Marcoux

Bonus Material #4:

Use Powerful Methods for Risks and Making Big Decisions

"It's hard for me to make the big decisions," my client Cara said.

"I hear you," I replied. "That's understandable. I've been listening carefully to your current situation and you have a lot at stake."

Working with clients, and as a CEO, leading my international team members for my own company, I work with people taking appropriate risks.

I recall this quote:

"Failure or the risk of failure could often be a crucial step on the road to success." – Dominic Randolph

Being skillful about "risk of failure" is valuable.

"The heart and soul of the company is creativity and innovation. ... People don't like to follow pessimists." – Bob Iger, CEO of The Walt Disney Company

I usually write about having courage and using strategy to take appropriate risks.

There is another side to this equation.

It's valuable to learn when taking a particular risk is ill-advised.

I use **3 Considerations Related to Saying "No" to a Particular Risk**

- "If It's not hell yes, then it's hell no."
- I don't feel a burning energy to do this.
- If in doubt, leave it out.
- *Bonus Consideration:* Really wanting it to be true does *not* make it true.

1. "If it's not hell yes, then it's hell no."

Years ago, I saw a comment by Cheryl Richardson in one of her books: "If it's not hell yes, then it's hell no."

This is useful. Why? Because whatever you decide, you're going to pay for it. For example, years ago, I directed a feature film in which I played a leading character and I did my own stunts.

I held onto the hood of a speeding, classic, cherry-red Chevy truck going 60 miles an hour.

Would I do that today? No. I'm not interested. Been there, done that. I'm older, and I'm *not* interested in risking great injury. I'd rather devote my time to leading my team in making six graphic novels of my series *Jack AngelSword*.

Now it's your turn. Do you really want something? Is it a total, enthusiastic "hell yes!"? If not, then maybe it's NOT worth it to you.

2. "I don't feel a burning energy to do this."

Recently, I was offered two big opportunities. Both required that I invest money and time in big proportions. I said to my sweetheart, "I don't feel a burning energy to do this." That was an important point! It's good to listen to yourself.

Now it's your turn. As you talk with people you trust about a particular risk, how do you REALLY feel about it? Do you feel a burning energy to do it?

3. If in doubt, leave it out

I've made big decisions. I've led five companies—plus directing my first feature film, giving my first big speech in front of 700 people, writing a book [I've written 41 books visible on Amazon.com], hiring important team members and more.

Did I have any doubts when I went ahead? I did have a small doubt or two. But during those times, my big, positive burning desire was more important than any fear I had.

On the other hand, a Big, Important Doubt, might be your intuition saying: "Hey! Pay attention to this. Something is OFF here."

If you have that kind of doubt, "leave it out"—that is, protect yourself and don't go down a dark path.

Now it's your turn. Do you have a "Big, Important Doubt"? Is your wish for a particular outcome maybe blinding you to a big downside?

3a. "Bonus": Really wanting it to be true does not make it true.

One particular time, someone invited me to join a business opportunity. When I first heard about the business situation and what MIGHT blossom out of it, my heart filled up with "Oh! I hope this is true—and this works! My life would change so much. This could be my Big Breakthrough!"

It was necessary for me to quiet down my fantasy-thoughts, and take a close look at the whole situation.

I call myself an OptiRealist. That is, I'm optimistic that we can make things better AND I'm realistic to know that strategy is necessary. Another realistic view is that any project can get bumpy or even fall apart. Maybe you could barely hold the project together, but with the wrong people involved, you could waste a lot of your time.

For example, I directed a particular film project years ago. A certain actor refused to re-record certain lines of dialogue. This person was afraid of losing close-up shots. Wait a minute! If the scene does not make sense, this actor would still lose!

I carefully explained the need for the scenes to be re-edited to make the whole film project work. Still, this actor refused to record new lines of dialogue.

My solution: I replaced the voice of that actor through the whole film. I had to fix the scenes. That was my job as producer and film director.

A Special Consideration: Ask yourself, "How much control do I have in the project so I can take action to fix things?" If you have multiple opportunities before you, you may want to focus on those projects that give you a good degree of control so you CAN fix things.

It is realistic to understand that sometimes people will be so self-focused that they may hurt a project.

My point is: Pay close attention. If you're in a project with trustworthy people, you'll be okay. If you doubt the professionalism of people involved, it may be time to avoid the deal or situation.

Now it's your turn. Have you interviewed a lot of people related to the proposed deal or situation? Have you made sure to realize "wanting something to be true does not make it true"?

As an Executive Coach and the Spoken Word Strategist, I often work with clients who need to take appropriate risks. How do you know if the risk is appropriate?

One part of the process is to thoroughly submit the risky deal or situation to these *3 Considerations Related to Saying "No" to a Particular Risk*

- "If It's not hell yes, then it's hell no."
- I don't feel a burning energy to do this.
- If in doubt, leave it out.
- *Bonus Consideration:* Really wanting it to be true does *not* make it true.

You really need to get access to your intuition. Some researchers identify intuition as "unconscious intelligence." That is, they suggest that you really KNOW something but it has not risen to the neocortex of the brain yet.

Pay close attention.

Guard your time and resources.

Then you can get the most value when you take an appropriate risk.

Principle: Make space for your intuition to alert you to elements both positive and negative.

Power Question: When you have a big decision to make do you listen to your own intuition?

Useful method: Use the Benjamin Franklin Method with a Twist. The classic Benjamin Franklin method involves: a) draw a vertical line down the center of a sheet of paper and b) list the PRO details of the decision on the left side and list the CON details on the right side. *Here's the "twist": Let your intuitive feelings tell you which of the details is most important.*

One time I wrote down 9 Pro details and then wrote 3 Con details. The third Con detail practically jumped off the page for me.

Later, my sweetheart said, "The reasons for the decision were like green peas. The one reason against the decision was like a watermelon."

Tom Marcoux

Bonus Material #5

Keep Your Dream Alive!

Recently, I had the opportunity to share the methods so *you can keep your dream alive.* Here's the text of that speech:

"I'm standing outside a door. In a couple of moments, I'm going to walk through that door, and I'm going to have a meeting with George Takei, that's Mr. Sulu of the original *STAR TREK.*

I'm excited. [Audience chuckles.]

I won't call myself a Trekkie, but I'll call myself a Trek Enthusiast.

For any Trekkers here, yes, I know he was promoted to Captain Sulu. [Audience chuckles.] So this is the original Mr. Sulu.

As I'm standing outside that door, I'm realizing "what did it take to come this far? How was I able to keep my dream alive and get to this level so I could ask this guy, 'Would you like to be an actor in my feature film?'"

What I realized is three main ideas. So I have three main ideas for you. The first idea is: **Express yourself.** This is tied in with **the benefits** that I'm bringing to you today. One is how to keep your dream alive. Two is how to persevere—how to keep going.

That's what I'm sharing with you, and I want to be of service and bring this to you.

The first main point is: Express Yourself—the beginning of all possibilities, *the beginning of all opportunities* is when you express yourself.

So, for my first visual aid: This is my first screenplay. This is how I broke into the film industry. It was written about two decades ago. It's called *LIVING*. As a screenplay, it's like a blueprint. You can't read it like a novel. You see how it has something like "code" on the page.

This is not a film. It's like a blueprint for a house.

This is where I began. I expressed myself. I was in my 20's and I decided to tell a story. One that I believed in, that I felt so deeply because I knew some people who were facing life-threatening illnesses ... You notice that this screenplay is called *LIVING*.

Also, at the time, between semesters, I was a day camp counselor. I can relate to Juliet (audience member) and being a teacher.

I was telling stories to the day camp children.

LIVING was a story I could tell from my own life experience. And I needed to tell it, I wanted to tell it. I wrote this screenplay; I expressed myself. And this was the beginning of my getting into the film industry.

I gave this screenplay to a software engineer. He gave it to another software engineer, who gave it to a real estate developer who gave it to the California Motion Picture Commissioner. He got me San Luis Obispo Airport. This is way before 911 [the attacks]. And he got me an American Eagle plane, both for free—because he believed in my writing.

This is point number one: Express Yourself—which leads us into point number two: *If you meet a roadblock, create a new road.*

The roadblock was the agent for Robin Williams.

Robin Williams is back in the news again; it breaks my heart. [News reports revealed the disease Robin had, which led to his death].

Still, twenty years ago, I wrote that screenplay, and I wanted Robin Williams to be the star of the feature film. So I gave the screenplay to his agent.

I don't remember his name, but the agent might as well have been called "Mr. Roadblock."

Mr. Roadblock said, "You must attach a solid offer to this screenplay."

How was I to give a solid offer? I was in my 20's. I'm just getting started.

What you need in the film industry is a triangle: Star, Good Screenplay and Director. That's how you make a movie.

I had a good screenplay. I'm trying to get the star. Mr. Roadblock got right in my way, and Robin Williams never saw my screenplay.

But if you meet a roadblock—what do we do?

[Audience says, "Create a new road."]

[Tom holds up a graphic novel titled *Crystal Pegasus*.] Here's my new road: This graphic novel called *Crystal Pegasus*.

The main character in my screenplay *LIVING* tells a story to day camp kids; the story is called "Crystal Pegasus."

This graphic novel is for children, their parents and grandparents.

You can see little Crystal Pegasus on the front of the graphic novel. That's his dear friend Rose, the dragon who has a rose imprinted on her chest.

Crystal Pegasus began as a young, small horse, and he woke up one morning and found out that he had wings!

Did the barnyard animals say, "Oh, fantastic! You have magic inside you, you manifested that as wings. This is great!"?

No. The barnyard animals, like some people and some

creatures do—they said, "I don't think those things belong to you so we're going to take them away!"

This scared the young horse. He ran; then he flew. But he wasn't very good at flying yet. BOOM!—he hit his head on a tree branch and fell—shheeeeeeesh—SPLASH! Into the Enchanted Lake.

The next morning, he found that he was now made of crystal. And like many of us, though he belonged in the sky, though he belongs creating and expressing himself—instead, he wouldn't fly because he was afraid that he would break! He's made of crystal.

This is a story about bravery, being true to yourself, stretching and flying. Also, it's about having good friends, eventually.

This is *Crystal Pegasus* and this is my new road. So I know because it's up on Amazon.com [Audience chuckles.]—I know that this can serve people.

I have not made my movie yet, but I can express something from it.

My first point was Express Yourself. My second point was: If you meet a roadblock, create a new road.

My third point is: Say Yes to Yourself.

We're conditioned, we're trained. We say yes to everybody. We say yes to the parents. We say yes to kids, family, friends. We say yes to the supervisor. We say yes to the customer. We say yes to everybody, and sometimes we find ourselves empty.

So we need you to say yes to yourself. So you can put some good joy inside. And happiness and energy *into* yourself.

You know that I wanted to tell this story in this *LIVING* screenplay for more than two decades.

Finally, I said yes to myself so the story of *LIVING* is now a novella inside this book [Tom holds up a paperback book titled *Droids to Magic: Fantastic Tales of Science Fiction and Wonder.*]

This book is a collection of my fiction. So 80 pages is the story of *LIVING*. A screenplay is a blueprint; you can't read it. But a novella, you can read.

So here it is. I have now expressed the *LIVING* story. So let me pull it all together for you.

We've talked about what it takes to persevere.

And we've talked about how to keep your dream alive.

So help me out here.

The first one, the beginning of everything is to:

[Audience says, "Express Yourself."]

Number two: If you meet that roadblock, you're going to

[Audience says, "Create a new road."]

And finally, this will lift your life, you

[Audience says, "Say Yes to Yourself."]

Thank you.

[Audience applauds.]

So with the text of my speech above, I've shared what it takes to persevere.

Principle: To persevere, stay flexible. If you meet a road block, create a new road.

Power Question: Have you tried a number of avenues to make your personal dream come true? Are you doing something new each year so you have NEW opportunities?

Bonus Material #6

Be Yourself, Continue Forward
Even When People Don't Hear You

"I overheard something that bothered me a lot," my client Amanda said. After a big breath, she continued, "I heard someone at my office say, 'Amanda said some self-aggrandizing stuff in her speech today.'"

A combination of sadness and panic came upon Amanda's face.

"What did I do wrong?!" Amanda said.

"I'm not sure that you did anything wrong. How about I ask you a couple of questions?" I asked.

"Okay."

"Did you tell the truth?"

"Yes."

"Were you making an important point?"

"Yes."

"Did you talk about something you learned?"

"Yes."

"Did you show how you went from making a mistake to succeeding at something?"

"Yes." Then Amanda's facial expression changed, and she said, "Oh …"

"Oh, what?"

"I don't think that person heard my whole story."

"Exactly!" I said, smiling.

In our discussion, I went onto point out:
- Sometimes, people don't hear your whole story. They get stuck on one detail.

- Sometimes, several people will never align with what you're talking about. And it's necessary to acknowledge that fact.

1. Sometimes, people don't hear your whole story. They get stuck on a detail.

I've noticed something recently. Sometimes, people literally do *not* hear one crucial word. Just yesterday, my sweetheart made a comment, and a friend, Joe, did not smile at her humorous detail.

I noticed this, and said, "Oh. She just added a funny detail about valium."

"Valium? Oh, I didn't hear that," Joe said.

Sometimes, people actually do not hear what you said. It can be a physical difficulty. Many of us have some form of damaged hearing due to loud music on mobile devices, concerts—and loud movie theaters.

Secondly, some people stop hearing you after one particular detail.

One of my clients, Wendy, told an audience of entrepreneurs that Bill Gates got a $50,000 loan from his father to buy an operating system that he renamed as MS-DOS. She discovered that many people tuned out because they felt that Bill Gates had been "born with a silver spoon in his mouth."

So the truth is: In every audience, you are likely to find that *some people never hear your whole story*. They get stuck on one detail, and then hear nothing more of what you express.

2. Sometimes, several people will never align with what you're talking about. And it's necessary to acknowledge that fact.

One of my mentors said, "If you even mention that you

wrote a book, some people in the audience will take offense."

"How?" I asked.

"Just by mentioning your book, to these particular individuals, you're selling something. And it bothers them. A lot," my mentor explained.

Ultimately, many of the top speakers in the world get to the point where they flow with the reality that they will always have people who miss the message they're offering.

"30% will love you. 30% will hate you. And 30% couldn't care less." – Gabrielle Reece

I add to the above comment with: "Do what you do. Don't let it stop you that 60% of the people may not be with you."

For a speaker, it's important to serve the 30% of the audience who are right there on the same page as you are. They ARE attentive. They want to learn.

* * * * * *

In recent weeks, my client Amanda has learned to set her own criteria for success.

She takes it in that when she gives a speech to 20 people and only two people have critical comments.

That's 18 people out of 20 who gained value.

That's good.

No—that's great!

You can still practice different ways to reach as many people as possible.

For example, I have trained speakers to reach analytical

people with a numbered list of methods. I've also guided them to have some friendly back-and-forth with audience members so that "relaters" (a personality style) can warm up to these speakers.

Be yourself.

Avoid becoming obsessed that some people did not hear you.

Practice methods to reach a spectrum of people.

Express what you've learned.

Do not toss your light under a garbage can just because some people cannot relate to your journey of learning and success.

Again—be yourself.

Principle: Some people get stuck and do NOT hear your whole story.

Power Question: Are you rehearsing in ways so you can reach different types of people? Additionally, are you learning to be okay with the fact that some people just cannot connect with what you're saying?

A Final Word and the Springboard to Your Dreams

Congratulations on your efforts with this book.

Please consider continuing to work with me through my **executive coaching** (phone and in-person), workshops and keynote addresses. Visit my blogs:

PitchPowerFest.com

BeHeadandBeTrusted.com

InstaMaxPro.com

YourBodySoulandProsperity.com

Meanwhile, *to get even more value from this book*, take the plans and insights that you created and place them in some form in your calendar or day planner. *Plan and take action*. Return to these pages again and again to reconnect with the material and take your life to higher levels.

The best to you,

Tom

Tom Marcoux

Executive Coach and Spoken Word Strategist

Pitch Coach

Special Offer Just for Readers of this Book:

Contact Tom Marcoux at tomsupercoach@gmail.com for special discounts on **coaching**, books, workshops and presentations. Just mention your experience with this book.

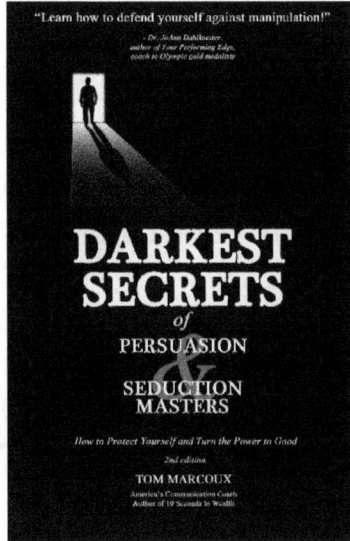

"Learn how to defend yourself against manipulation!"
— Dr. JoAnn Dahlkoetter,
author of Your Performing Edge,
coach to Olympic gold medalists

DARKEST SECRETS
of
PERSUASION
&
SEDUCTION
MASTERS

How to Protect Yourself and Turn the Power to Good

2nd edition

TOM MARCOUX
America's Communication Coach
Author of 10 Seconds to Wealth

Excerpt from

Darkest Secrets of Persuasion and Seduction Masters: How to Protect Yourself and Turn the Power to Good

by Tom Marcoux, Executive Coach – Spoken Word Strategist

Copyright Tom Marcoux

. . . Now, I am in my 40's, with gray in my hair, and for 27 years I have been taking action to protect people.

And now is the time for me to protect you with the Countermeasures I reveal in this book.

Every human being needs to be able to break the trance that a Manipulator creates. You need to make good decisions so you are safe and you keep growing—and you are not cut down and crippled.

This Darkest Secrets material is so intense that I first released it only with the counterbalance of my most energizing and uplifting books, *Soar! Nothing Can Stop You This Year* and *Year of Awesome: How You Can Use 12 Success Principles including 10 Seconds to Wealth.*

An interviewer asked me: "Who can be the Manipulator?"

A co-worker, a boss, a salesperson, someone you're dating, and someone you think is a friend.

Now is the time—this very minute—for me to write this book to protect you.

I must speak the truth.

These Darkest Secrets of "persuasion masters" are ...

Wait a minute! Let's say it plainly: These are the Darkest Secrets of masters of manipulation. Throughout this book, I will call these people what they are: Manipulators.

Dictionary.com defines "manipulate" as "To influence or manage shrewdly or deviously.... To tamper with or falsify for personal gain."

In this book, we will look on a manipulator as one who deviously influences someone with no concern about that person's well-being, and who causes harm to that person.

Here is the first Darkest Secret:

Darkest Secret #1:

Manipulators Make You Hurt

and Then Offer the Salve.

Manipulators would invite you to go out in the sun for hours and then sell you the salve to soothe your burns. The problem is that we don't notice that this is what they're doing.

For example, you're considering the purchase of a house. A Manipulator asks the question, "So, where would you put your TV?" This question is designed to put you into a trance.

Dictionary.com defines "trance" as "a half-conscious state, seemingly between sleeping and waking, in which ability to function voluntarily may be suspended." Let's condense this: in a trance you may not be able to function freely.

Here is the second Secret:

Darkest Secret #2:

Manipulators Put You into a Trance.

To protect yourself, you must learn to use Countermeasures to Break the Trance.

All the Countermeasures (actions you can take to break the trance) in this book will make you stronger and more capable of protecting yourself.

Now, we'll view the third Secret:

Darkest Secret #3:

Manipulators Care Nothing for You and Human Decency: They'll lie, cheat, and do whatever they need to do so they win—but their charm masks all this.

Let's return to the example of a Manipulator selling you a house. A Manipulator does not pause for an instant to see if you can truly afford the new house. The Manipulator would neglect to mention that you will not only have your mortgage payment of $900. There will be additional costs: home repairs, property tax, water, electricity, homeowner's insurance, and more. The Manipulator only emphasizes what he or she knows you want to hear: "Look! $900 is better than the $1500 you're paying for rent, which is just going down the toilet. And the $900 is an investment."

Let's go back to **Darkest Secret #1:**

Manipulators make you hurt and then offer the salve.

The Manipulator has you feeling good about the solution (salve) and feeling bad about your current life situation.

How? A Manipulator will make you hurt through questions such as:

• What bothers you about paying $1500 a month for rent? (The Manipulator will use a derisive tone when he says the word rent.)

• What is not smart about paying rent on someone else's house instead of investing in your own house?

• How do you feel about your children walking in the

neighborhood where you live now?

Do you see how these questions are designed to make you hurt enough so that you'll buy?

An interviewer asked me, "Tom, aren't these good arguments for purchasing a house?"

"What we're looking at is the *intention* of the influencer," I replied. "Let's look at our definition of a manipulator as one who deviously influences someone with no concern about that person's well-being, and who causes harm to that person. If the person truly cannot afford the house, he or she will be harmed by buying it. If the manipulator conceals the truth, the manipulator is doing harm. That's the important difference."

Some friends of mine are ethical and helpful real estate agents who truthfully reveal the whole situation and help the purchaser achieve her own goals.

In this book, we are talking about another type of person; that is, unethical Manipulators.

* * *

In any given moment, we need to remember the tactics Manipulators use. We will focus on the word D.A.R.K. so you can remember details easily and protect yourself from Manipulators.

D — Dangle something for nothing

A — Alert to scarcity

R — Reveal the Desperate Hot Button

K — Keep on pushing buttons

1. Dangle Something for Nothing

What do conmen and conwomen do to seize your attention? They make you think you're getting a "steal."

I recently saw a documentary in which a conman on a street in England showed a toy that looked like it was dancing. This fake product was actually dancing because of a hidden, invisible thread. The conman was dangling something for nothing. The Entranced Buyer thought he was getting something worth $20 for only $5. That was the trick. The Entranced Buyer felt that he was getting $15 extra of value for his $5. What the Buyer really got was something worth nothing. Similarly, I know someone who purchased a copy of a Disney movie from a street vendor in San Francisco. She brought the copy home and it was unwatchable—and the street vendor was never seen again.

An old phrase goes, "A conman cannot con someone who is not looking for something for nothing."

How to Protect Yourself from "Dangle Something for Nothing"

Stop! Get on your cell phone and talk through the "deal" with someone you know who thinks clearly. Go home. Think about it. Do some research on the Internet. Listen to your gut feelings. If the salesman or conman is too insistent, get away from that Manipulator. Get quiet. Have a cup of water. Cool down. Break the Trance!

Break the Trance and Identify the Crucial Detail

Earlier, I mentioned that a Manipulator puts you into a trance. An added problem is that we put ourselves into a trance. For example, as you read this, are you thinking about your right toe? Most likely not (unless you stubbed your toe recently). The point is that we only focus on a tiny percentage of what is going on in our life.

Around fifteen years ago, I caused myself trouble because I put myself into a trance. I discovered that under certain conditions, friendship can make you nearly deaf. Here's how: I was producing a song for a motion picture. A good friend was singing backup in the chorus. Because of our friendship, I wanted him to sound great. I completely missed the Crucial Detail. In this kind of situation, the Crucial Detail is that what truly counts is how the lead singer sounds! I made a song that I could not release. What a waste of time and money! I had put myself into a trance.

In any situation in which the Manipulator is "dangling something for nothing," we often fall into a trance and miss the Crucial Detail. The most important detail is *not* that we're saving money if we order before midnight tonight. What counts is whether the product creates a lasting, crucial benefit in our lives. And is the benefit of the product worth the cost? Some people even program themselves to make mistakes by saying, "I can't pass up a bargain." The bargain is *not* the Crucial Detail.

Secrets to Break the Trance

This is the process of B.R.E.A.K.S. It will help you remember the proven methods to break a trance.

B — Breathe

R — Relax

E — Envision

A — Act on aromas

K — Keep moving

S — Smile

Secret #1: Breathe

Remember Secret #1: Manipulators make you hurt and then offer the salve. The Manipulator wants to put you into a state of being that fills you with a sense of urgency and anxiety. Oh, no! I'm going to miss the sale!

Stop this highly vulnerable state. Take a deep breath.

End of Excerpt from

Darkest Secrets of Persuasion and Seduction Masters: How to Protect Yourself and Turn the Power to Good

Purchase your copy of this book (paperback or eBook) at Amazon.com or BarnesandNoble.com

See **Free Chapters** of Tom Marcoux's 41 books at http://amzn.to/ZiCTRj

ABOUT THE AUTHOR

You want more and better, right? Imagine fulfilling your Big Dream.

Tom Marcoux can help you—in that he's coached thousands of people: CEOs, small business leaders, graduate students (at Stanford University) speakers, and authors.

Marcoux is known as an effective **Executive Coach** and **Spoken Word Strategist.**

(and Thought Leader—okay, writing 41 books helped with that!)

** *CEOs, Vice-Presidents, Other Executives, Small Business Leaders:*

You know that leading people and speaking at your best can be tough.

Marcoux solves problems while helping you amplify your own Charisma, Confidence and Control of Time.

Interested? Email Marcoux—tomsupercoach@gmail.com

Ask for a *Special Report:*

* 9 Deadly Mistakes to Avoid for Your Next Speech

** *Speakers, Experts—for a great TED Talk, Book, Audio Book, Speeches, YouTube Videos.*

Marcoux solve problems while helping you to make your Concise, Compelling Message that gets people to trust you and get what you're offering (product, service, *an idea*).

Marcoux is the founder of **PitchPowerFest.com**

Yes—the *San Francisco Examiner* designated Tom Marcoux

as "The Personal Branding Instructor."

As a **Pitch Coach**, Marcoux is an expert on STORY. He won a Special Award at the EMMY AWARDS, and he directed a feature film that went to the CANNES FILM MARKET and earned international distribution.

(Marcoux helps you *be heard and be trusted*—a focus point of his 16th Anniversary edition book, *Connect: High Trust Communication for Your Success in Business and Life*.)

As a CEO, Marcoux leads teams in the United Kingdom, India and the USA. Marcoux guides clients & audiences (IBM, Sun Microsystems, etc.) in "Soar with Confidence", leadership, team-building, power time management and branding. See Tom's Popular BLOG:

www.TomSuperCoach.com

Specialties: coach to CEOS * Executives * Small Business owners * Leaders * Speakers * Experts * Authors * Academics

One of his *Darkest Secrets* books rose to #1 on Amazon.com Hot New Releases in Business Life (and in Business Communication). A member of the National Speakers Association for over 15 years, Marcoux is a professional coach and guest expert on TV, radio, and print.

Marcoux addressed National Association of Broadcasters' Conference six years running. With a degree in psychology, he is a guest lecturer at **Stanford University**, DeAnza, & California State University. Over the years, Marcoux has taught business communication, designing careers, public speaking, science fiction cinema/literature and comparative religion at Academy of Art University. He is engaged in book/film projects *Crystal Pegasus* (children's) and *Jack AngelSword* (thriller-fantasy). See Tom's well-received blogs at

BeHeardandBeTrusted.com

PitchPowerFest.com

YourBodySoulandProsperity.com

InstaMaxPro.com

Consider engaging **Tom Marcoux as your Executive Coach.**

"As Tom's client for many years, I have benefited from his wisdom and strategic approach. Do your career and personal life a big favor and get his books and engage him as **your Executive Coach**." – Dr. JoAnn Dahlkoetter, author of *Your Performing Edge* and Coach to CEOs and Olympic Gold Medalists

"Tom Marcoux coached me to get more done in 10 days than other coaches in 2 years." – Brad Carlson, CEO of MindStrong LLC

As the Spoken Word Strategist, Tom Marcoux can help you with **speech writing** and **coaching for your best performance.**

As the founder of **PitchPowerFest.com** and as a **Pitch Coach**, Tom trains CEOs, entrepreneurs and business owners to make **compelling pitches** to gain funding, key team members and powerful advisors.

As Tom says, *Make Your Speech a Pleasant Beach.*

Join Tom's Linkedin.com group: *Executive Public Speaking and Communication Power.*

At Google+: join the community "Create Your Best Life – Charisma & Confidence"

Get a **Free** report: "9 Deadly Mistakes to Avoid for Your Next Speech and 9 Surefire Methods" at

http://tomsupercoach.com/freereport9Mistakes4Speech.html

Tom Marcoux has trained CEOs, small business owners,

and graduate students to speak with impact and gain audiences' tremendous approval and cooperation. *Learn how to present and get thunderous applause!*

"Tom, Thanks for your coaching and work with me on revising my speech at a major university. Working with you has been so enlightening for me. Through your gentle prodding and guidance, I was able to write a speech that connects with the audience. I wish everyone could experience the transformation I have undergone. You have helped me discover the warm and compelling stories that now make my speech reach hearts and uplift minds. This was truly an empowering experience. I cannot thank you enough for your great assistance." — J.S.

- **"Tom Marcoux has been an NAB Conference favorite [speaker] for six years. And he is very energetic." – John Marino, Vice President, National Assn. of Broadcasters, Washington, D.C.**

- **"Using just one of Tom Marcoux's methods, I got more done in 2 weeks than in 6 months." – Jaclyn Freitas, M.A.**

Tom's Coaching features innovations:
- Dynamic Rehearsal
- Power Rehearsal for Crisis
- The Charisma Advantage that Saves You Time

Become a fan of Tom's graphic novels/feature films:

- Fantasy Thriller: *Jack AngelSword*
  type "JackAngelSword" at Facebook.com

- YA Fiction: *Jenalee Storm*
  At Facebook.com type: "JenaleeStorm"

- Science fiction: *TimePulse*
  www.facebook.com/timepulsegraphicnovel

- Children's Fantasy: *Crystal Pegasus*
  www.facebook.com/crystalpegasusandrose

See **Free Chapters** of Tom Marcoux's 41 books
at http://amzn.to/ZiCTRj   Amazon.com

www.ingramcontent.com/pod-product-compliance
Lightning Source LLC
Chambersburg PA
CBHW060607210326
41519CB00014B/3593